# Physical Characteristi~ ~~
# Bergamasco
## (from the Fédération Cynologique Internat

CW00493258

**Body:** The Bergamasco is very slightly lo..~ ..... .....

**Tail:** Set on last third of rump, thick and strong at its root, tapering towards its extremity. Covered with goat-like hair.

**Hindquarters:** Limbs straight, as much in profile as from behind.

**Coat:** Texture typical of this breed is the presence of three types of hair: the undercoat, fine, dense and oily, adhering to the skin and forming a water-proof, protective layer; the goat hair, strong and rough as in goats and which stays smooth without tuft-ing; and the woolly coat, finer in texture which grows together in flocks. The "flock" should be larger at its base, flat, irregular and sometimes opening fan-wise.

**Color:** The coat color is gray of all possible shades, from a most delicate gray to black.

**Feet:** Front feet are oval shaped with well closed and arched toes. Rear feet are the same as the front ones except slightly smaller.

# Bergamasco

By Maria Andreoli and Donna DeFalcis

# CONTENTS

KENNEL CLUB BOOKS: **BERGAMASCO**
**ISBN: 1-59378-315-9**

Copyright © 2004
Kennel Club Books, Inc., 308 Main Street, Allenhurst, NJ 07711 USA
Cover Design Patented: US 6,435,559 B2 • Printed in South Korea

PHOTOGRAPHS BY ISABELLE FRANÇAIS AND CAROL ANN JOHNSON
with additional photos by Norvia Behling, T.J. Calhoun,
Carolina Biological Supply, David Dalton, Doskocil, James Hayden-Yoav,
James R. Hayden, RBP, Bill Jonas, Dwight R. Kuhn, Dr. Dennis Kunkel,
Mikki Pet Products, Phototake, Jean Claude Revy,
Dr. Andrew Spielman and Alice van Kempen.

ILLUSTRATIONS BY PATRICIA PETERS.

*The publisher wishes to thank the authors
and all of the other owners of the dogs featured in this book.*

At the end of the 19th century, the Bergamasco was still referred to as the Alpine Sheepdog and the Northern Italian Sheepdog. The breed's official name is a fairly recent designation.

# BERGAMASCO

## ORIGIN OF THE BREED

It is now universally accepted that the first centers for domestication of sheep and goats were located in central and southern Asia. From these regions, populations that migrated in search of new pastures from east to west settled in mountainous zones along a practically uninterrupted line from the upper plains of Asia across the mountains of Anatolia, the Caucasus, the Carpathians and the Alps to the Pyrenees.

Scientists who dedicated their studies to cow- and sheep-breeding noted the presence, in these same regions, of dogs with long, bristly coats. The origins of these breeds probably go back to the Himalayan zones, where there existed a wolf known as *Canis lupus laniger,* which had a very thick coat. Along this route there are a number of dog breeds now stabilized and recognized, which are almost certainly direct descendants from a common ancestor. From a historical point of view, it is quite logical that a group of dog breeds with such similarities is to be found along the routes followed by these migrant populations.

The characteristics shared by all of these dogs are robust constitutions and thick, rough coats with more or less pronounced tendencies to felting on all parts of the body, including on the head, where the hair often forms a curtain in front of the eyes. These characteristics have become set, due to the dogs' adaptation to the climates and geographical locations of their places of origin, and maintained through environmental conditions. The breeds that are known today for these characteristics are the Ovcharka in Russia, the Komondor and Puli in Hungary, the Polish Lowland Sheepdog in Poland, the Sheeppoedel in Germany (now very rare but not entirely extinct), the Bergamasco in the Italian Alps, the Briard and the Berger des Pyrenees (Little Pyrenean Sheepdog) in the French Alps and the Catalan Sheepdog in the Spanish Pyrenees.

A migratory current far further north could have been responsible for the presence of other dog breeds, probably of the same origin as the aforementioned—the Old English Sheepdog (Bobtail), which is still a working breed in northern England and the Scottish Highlands, and the Bearded Collie in Britain. There is also mention of a Norwegian Sheepdog of days gone by.

Once these migratory populations abandoned their nomadic existence and settled down

Many shepherds consider the Bergamasco as an ideal breed for handling sheep. Even the sheep seem to respect them as they wait attentively for the dog's "instructions."

within confined territories, their inseparable companions, their dogs, underwent the same evolution. Together with their masters, the dogs settled down in all parts of Europe and lost contact with groups located elsewhere. Climatic conditions, environmental factors and the habits of the local populations with whom they lived influenced the evolution of these isolated groups in varying manners so that, with the passing of the centuries, their looks, character and habits underwent changes. Each one of these groups of dog assumed its own identity, which made it different from its remote ancestor, but also different from the dogs of other groups. However, even today, these differences are not so great that we cannot recognize the different breeds' common origin.

The ancestors of our modern Bergamasco arrived in Italy, spreading right over the flanks of the Alps. Until some 50 to 60 years ago, when sheep breeding was still prevalent in much of northern Italy, the dog was to be found throughout the entire Alpine region. Initially, our Bergamasco must have been used as a watchdog, which constituted the original function of the breed and remained unchanged over the centuries. Originally, all sheepdogs were guard dogs, and their activity was limited to

**GENUS *CANIS***
Dogs and wolves are members of the genus *Canis*. Wolves are known scientifically as *Canis lupus* while dogs are known as *Canis domesticus*. Dogs and wolves are known to interbreed. The term "canine" derives from the Latin-derived word *Canis*. The term "dog" has no scientific basis but has been used for thousands of years. The origin of the word "dog" has never been authoritatively ascertained.

protecting the flocks from animals of prey. The guard dog carries out his task by remaining close to the flock, and his instinct makes him immediately aware of the approach of strangers, human or animal, that attempt to penetrate the imaginary protective circle that the dog has drawn around the flock. The guardian sheepdog was and is still now used to protect the flock, and no other kind of work is expected from this type of dog.

However, in regions where agriculture progressively was developing, the process of stock-breeding needed to adapt to changing conditions. Forests were being cleared and areas previously dedicated to grazing were being ploughed up, thus restricting the territory available for wild animals and limiting their numbers. The continuous disappearance of wide open spaces for grazing necessitated important changes in the time-honored traditions of stock-breeding.

Before the advent of wide-scale agriculture, the flocks were able to wander from one grazing ground to another without demographic barriers, so that their roaming did not need to be controlled. Once these zones were under cultivation, what had once been no-man's land became the property of individuals who defended their land against intruders. It therefore became difficult to cross these zones. To avoid problems, it became necessary to drive the flocks over restricted passages and to make certain that the animals did not trespass. The classic methods used by shepherds for keeping their flocks together proved inadequate. It was at this point that men realized how better use of their dogs could be an advantage to them.

This transformation was no more than a gradual and slow evolution during which the dog retained his guardian qualities, but also acquired a new behavior pattern through which he learned to drive the flock. These methods had never been applied

to the ferocious guard dogs, as it would have been dangerous to deliberately set them after the sheep when it might not be possible to curb their aggression. They were, therefore, gradually replaced by smaller, friendlier dogs with great intelligence. This transformation process was slow, progressive and, in the beginning at least, unintentional. These circumstances were what gradually led toward increased use of the sheepdog.

Since this extended function (meaning the dogs' ability to herd) was required sooner or later in many different places, particularly in Europe, it is impossible to confine the dogs' evolution to one place or to one moment in time. This new behavior pattern could only have been acquired and ingrained over a long evolutionary period due to rigid selection. Although scarce, we can find traces of this evolutionary process of our dogs amid historical data, providing us with a significant guideline.

Of particular importance was the migration of Italian sheep to Switzerland, which commenced in the latter Middle Ages (the first documentation refers to the year AD 739) and continued until 1886, when the Swiss government banned it. From the eastern Piedmont and Lombardy regions, the flocks crossed the Valtellina and the more accessible of the

Capable of both guarding and herding, the Bergamasco is a one-dog shepherding system.

Alpine passes to reach the Grisons, where summer pasturelands were leased for them. The sheep migrated in vast numbers, some reports indicating as many 40,000 heads. Surely shepherds needed the help of the sheepdogs to accomplish this migration.

In ancient times, the Alpine passes were wild areas where bears and wolves lived. Large and ferocious guardian sheepdogs were essential for the protection of flocks and men. The writings of G. von Albertini von Tamins, dated 1781, inform us that at the beginning of June, Italian shepherds drove their flocks up the Splugen Pass from Piedmont. He continues, saying that their excellent sheepdogs not only bravely guarded their masters and the flocks against wolves but also nearly replaced the shepherds in managing the animals. This is the first citation that confirms the beginning of the transition from watchdog to drover. In books written some years later, we find descriptions of these sheepdogs: "Big dogs with long, woolly coats are the courageous assistants of the Bergamasco Shepherds" and "...large thin with long, woolly coats."

Influenced also by environmental changes, the character and habits of the dogs progressively adapted. In the Hoepli manual of 1897, *The Dog*, author

Angelo Vecchi stated, "The North Italian Sheepdog, in particular those that emanate from the Alpine regions, are docile, friendly and not aggressive unless their flocks are menaced. The shepherds teach them how to manage the sheep to prevent them from straying into fields along the paths they follow on their long journeys and to keep them together on roads."

It is interesting to note that, around the end of the 19th century, the dog was still defined by some authors as "Alpine Sheepdog" and sometimes as "Northern Italian Sheepdog," proving that the name "Bergamasco Sheepdog" is fairly recent. The present name should not be attributed to its place of origin, as is commonly assumed, but is more probably linked to the history of the "traveling shepherds." The arid Bergamasco Valleys provided few resources for the inhabitants, who were thus forced to seek work elsewhere. These men now became salaried shepherds who took care of the flocks of rich landowners and whose work consisted of driving the flocks to the most suitable pastures. These traveling shepherds, as indicated by their name, followed the migratory routes that took them from the high Swiss plains to the shores of rivers in the Po Valley, according to the season and other requirements. This work was traditionally carried out by

The Bergamasco is tolerant of all kinds of "kids." They are very docile and friendly unless called upon to protect their human families or their herds.

people from the Bergamasco Valleys, so that, due to their association with the dogs that always accompanied them, it is highly probable that the name "Bergamasco," which referred to the shepherds, also became the common name of the dogs.

For us, the important thing to remember is that we must not be confused by the breed's name and consider the Bergamasco region as its home territory. To obtain a Bergamasco Sheepdog, you must not think that you will find it among the shepherds in those mountainous valleys, since sheep have long ago left that region. Industrial expansion and the development of tourism caused profound economic changes in lifestyle in the Alpine valleys. Victims of this transition were the flocks, together with their guardian dogs. No longer jealously protected by their shepherd masters, the dogs gradually disappeared or were mongrelized. Greater communication facilities favored the infiltration of new breeds into the previously isolated regions where the only dogs with the right of existence had been the ones useful for the shepherds' work. It is only thanks to the efforts of a few enthusiastic breeders that it has been possible, after a long period of decline, to restore consistency and homogeneity to this Italian breed. In view of its

**NOT "CORDED"**
The Bergamasco does not have a corded coat like a Hungarian Puli or Komondor; rather, their hair creates "flocks" or "maps," from the Italian word *biocolli*.

exceptional qualities, the Bergamasco can now compete on equal footing with the best-known foreign breeds.

**DEVELOPMENT OF THE BREED ON THE CONTINENT**
The birth of Alpino di Valle Imagna, the dog that was the progenitor of the breed on the Continent, has very humble beginnings, tracing to a poor shepherd who happened upon the farm of Mr. Rota in the Bergamasco hills in the late 1940s or early 1950s. The shep-

herd's dam was about to deliver her puppies, and the shepherd requested permission to leave the bitch on the farm until she birthed the pups. She delivered two very lovely puppies, one of which Mr. Rota chose to keep; this was the puppy that grew up

## BRAIN AND BRAWN

Since dogs have been inbred for centuries, their physical and mental characteristics are constantly being changed to suit man's desires for hunting, retrieving, scenting, guarding and warming their masters' laps. During the past 150 years, dogs have been judged according to physical characteristics as well as functional abilities. Few breeds can boast a genuine balance between physique, working ability and temperament like the Bergamasco can.

to become Alpino di Valle Imagna.

A businessman from Milan, Mr. Rota became increasingly interested in the breed as Alpino grew up, and he, together with his friend who kept Alpino's litter sister, went to various meeting places of the local shepherds to find other Bergamasco-type dogs. With the dogs they were able to find, the Valle Imagna Kennel officially began breeding the Bergamasco.

In little time, other kennels sprouted up, including Idro, Lupercali, Valle Scrivia, Albera and Grigiastro, many of which were based on the Valle Imagna bloodlines. An important kennel was founded in Switzerland by Mrs. Maria Schreiber, who lived in England, where many Italian flocks migrated for the summer months. With the flocks came also the intelligent Bergamasco Sheepdogs, which were quite recognizable in certain areas of Britain. Charmed by the cleverness of these dogs in working the flocks, Mrs. Schreiber came to Italy to meet Mr. Rota and to buy a bitch from his foundation dog, Alpino. This was the beginning of the Dimgod Kennel, which for many years yielded many important dogs. Mrs. Schreiber always remained in contact with the Italian breeders, especially the Valle Scrivia and Albera Kennels, with whom she enjoyed

In Italian, the breed is referred to as the *Pastore Bergamasco*.

cooperative relationships.

Among the newer kennels that were founded in Italy and remain in operation are Antica Priula, Pierzez and Val Brembana. Other Italian kennels were established, though many ceased operation after some time had passed.

Alpino von Dimgod and Icnusa dell'Albera were the founders of the Bergamin's Kennel in Holland. Mr. and Mrs. Beenen, who campaigned their dogs at the most important shows in Europe, receive credit for popularizing the Bergamasco in northern Europe.

In more recent times, the Bergamasco has expanded beyond the Italian pastures to other European nations, which have finally begun to embrace this marvelous Italian dog as their own. In Switzerland came the Arcobaleno and Monte-vergine Kennels, the latter of which is based on old Italian bloodlines of working dogs. In Germany, Mr. and Mrs. Papen-brock are the owners of Lopautal Kennel, which produced the bitch who won World Champion at the World Dog Show in Milan in 2000. In the Czech Republic, the Ätefika Kennel of Mr. Peter Ätefika promises many great Bergamascos to the world, especially now that certain political tensions have dissolved, allow-

Facing page: The Dell'Albera strain can be proud of Gae Dell'Albera Silver Streak, who won her American Rare Breed Association championship.

ing this kennel to communicate more freely with other breeders around Europe.

In recent years, the Bergamasco was introduced to the Scandinavian countries. In Finland, Kirsi and Jyri Ansamaki are promoting the breed through their Fallenhaus Kennel to Eastern European nations, including Russia, Estonia and Lithuania. The Rastafellow Kennel is the first of the newer kennels to be developed in this part of the Continent. In Sweden, the Bautastenen Kennel of Mr. and Mrs. Quick and the Frosta Kennel of Mrs. Gunvor Bergström are working hard to introduce the Bergamasco into their country, where the breed is completely unknown. One puppy from the Frosta Kennel went to Norway in hopes of promoting the breed in that country.

**THE BERGAMASCO SHEEPDOG IN BRITAIN**

The authors extend their gratitude to Reyna G. Knight of the Chique Kennels for information about the breed in the United Kingdom.

Mr. and Mrs. J. Webb were the first to own a Bergamasco in England. This Bergamasco was named La Donna Grigia of Triskele and was, of course, a bitch. Whelped on February 28, 1989, Donna, bred by N.

Fabrizio, was out of a dam named Nera and sired by Baldo. Genetically black, she was gray in color.

The author, Maria Andreoli, exported England's second Bergamasco to the UK in 1991. Ammone Dell'Albera of Chique, after six months in quarantine, came to his new owners, Mr. and Mrs. D. Knight. His sire was Ratafià Dell'Albera and his dam was Runcina Dell'Albera. Black in color, Ammone was born on April 23, 1990.

Ammone is credited with siring the first litter in England, and, of course, Donna was the first dam to deliver. As the fates would have it, on the very day that Ammone was released from the quarantine station, his "donna"-in-waiting was ready for mating. It was a rather brief courtship, but the happy result was eight black puppies.

On December 31, 1994, four gray puppies, sired by Int. Ch. Zecchino Dell'Albera out of Ubi Dell'Albera, were born in quarantine. Two of each sex, the puppies, bringing Britain's total Bergamasco population to 14, were named Dell'Albera Elisir D'Amore of Chique, Dell'Albera Effetto Speciale, Dell'Albera Erbavoglio and Dell'Albera Eclissi di Luna. After 12 weeks at the quarantine kennel, the gray four became part of England's active Bergamasco

troupe, being shown at the dog shows. Ubi, the sire, did not remain in the UK; he returned to Italy.

From Ammone and Donna's original litter of eight, Triskele Zamico, owned by K. I. and A. T. Sear, was also shown regularly, along with two others from that litter, though less frequently. In 1998, Igea dell'Albera, bred by the author, Maria Andreoli, entered the United Kingdom, happily side-stepping the six-month quarantine law due to the Balai Agreement.

The Bergamascos in the UK are exhibited at English Kennel Club shows in the Import Register, which prohibits them from competing in any other class and Best in Show. When Donna, the country's first dog, entered the UK, she competed in the Rare Breed category and, thereby, could be seen in the Best in Show ring as well as in the Stakes classes. Since the early 1990s, The Kennel Club has changed its policy; thus, Bergamascos are quite limited at the shows and, of course, cannot compete at the prestigious Crufts Dog Show since only qualified champions can compete in that show. Fortunately, however, the breed can be present in the Import Register, and thus are able to be seen by the thousands who visit the Crufts show. Once the breed establishes that it is "sufficient in number" and has "a good gene pool," The Kennel Club will permit the Bergamasco to enter and compete in the Championship Classes at all of its shows.

At the Windsor Championship Dog Show in 1995, seven Bergamascos were entered in the Import Register Classes. This represented 50 percent of the country's Bergamasco population—quite a fine turnout percentage-wise. Mr. L. Pagliero judged and placed Elisir D'Amour Dell'Albera of Chique first in the Puppy Class. Since then, the Bergamasco has been seen at most of the country's Championship Shows and Open Shows where Import Classes are offered. The Bergamascos have claimed many Best Puppy and Best Import awards.

In 1996, the Committee of the National Working Breeds hosted a breed seminar for 100 Kennel Club judges, which was conducted by Reyna G. Knight, who was elected the first chairman of the newly formed Bergamasco Club of Great Britain the following year. Mr. Stuart Band became the club's first secretary.

## THE BERGAMASCO IN THE US

Mr. and Mrs. Byfield imported the first Bergamasco into the United States. Marco, as he was called, was sent by Mrs. Byfield's brother, who lived in Italy. A bitch was later imported, and at least one litter was produced by the Byfields. Today, the Byfields live with two senior Bergamascos who are still active at 13 years of age. Unfortunately, no records were kept either of the ownership or the location of the puppies they produced.

Co-author Donna DeFalcis had never encountered a Bergamasco, but became intrigued by the breed's appearance through photographs she had seen of Bergamascos. She and her husband Stephen were trying to find a breed that was still in its original state, unchanged for the purposes of dog showing. Temperament and close family ties were their goals for their new breed.

With some hopes of establishing the breed in the US from the Dell'Albera line, which already touted a number of International Champions, in July 1995 they imported Fauno Dell'Albera, a six-month-old gray male, to join their family of two Polish Lowland Sheepdogs, Cole and Cody. They registered their Italian import, Fauno Dell'Albera, with the FCI as well as with the American Kennel Club's Foundation Stock Service. Understanding commands only in Italian, the newly arrived Fauno possessed a good-sized head, an agile body of medium build and a soft woolly coat with multiple shades of gray and black. He also had some black patches, which helped him acquire his call name, "Blackfoot." Soon Fauno's show-ring career and English-language education began as he entered the show circuit, introducing many rare-breed people to the Bergamasco.

By the time he reached two years of age, Fauno was a champion of several rare-breed clubs and had garnered multiple Best in

## ASSOCIATION INFORMATION

The International Bergamasco Sheepdog Association (IBSA) can be located on the Internet at **pastore-bergamasco.org**. IBSA is a source of international information for fanciers around the world. Its stated purpose is to provide accurate information about the breed, clubs and breeders to everyone interested in the breed.

Show awards, becoming one of the top 100 winning dogs in the American Rare Breed Association (ARBA).

In March 1996, the DeFalcises went to Italy to pick up Gae Dell'Albera, a four-month-old black bitch, whose genetic background was selected to enhance and preserve Fauno's characteristics in his offspring. At 18 months of age, Gae possessed a somewhat slighter body and overall size than Fauno, but she is just as beautiful in conformation, temperament and movement. As a puppy she won Best in Show, and she is more than willing to show her spirit in the show arena. She, too, is an ARBA champion, and she has also begun some herding tests along with Fauno.

In June 1998, Gae and Fauno Dell'Albera had a litter of eight puppies, five black and three gray, four males and four females. This litter of eight puppies was the first registered litter of Bergamascos within North America. The breeders did not retain any of these puppies, but sent them all off to worthy families who anxiously awaited their new Bergamascos.

In September 1998, the DeFalcises acquired Latria Dell'Albera, a six-month-old black female. She is a lovely bitch on the smaller side of the standard and as alert as they come. Her call name fast became "The Silver Dancer."

Although a bit aloof, it did not take her much time to win the hearts of the entire DeFalcis household, including three teenage boys, whom she accepted after a year of living with the family. A few months after The Silver Dancer stepped into the DeFalcises' lives, so also did Lindoro Dell'Albera, a light-gray male, sent from Italy at six months of age. He was gentle and graceful, appearing to float as he trotted, even at the young age of six months. His structure is a bit smaller than that of Fauno, but this dog too adds much to the American gene pool of the Bergamasco breed.

The fifth Bergamasco arrived, this time from England. Clothos is a light-gray male who arrived at four months age. Clothos arrived when Gae and Lindoro had a litter of ten puppies, and he quickly became the puppies' surrogate playmate and confidante.

By the year 2000, there were over 30 registered Bergamascos throughout the US and Canada. To serve the needs of this growing population, Donna and Stephen DeFalcis founded the Bergamasco Sheepdog Club of America. The club's first priority is to preserve and recognize the Bergamasco in its original state, properly acknowledging the breed's 2000-year heritage as the progenitor of many breeds that are known throughout Europe and the US.

Italian import Gae Dell'Albera Silver Blackfoot has won many Best in Show awards, including this one at ARBA when she was still a puppy.

The appeal and popularity of the Bergamasco is growing world-wide. This is the first Bergamasco gathering at the Cherry Blossom show of the American Rare Breed Association held in Washington, DC in 1999.

# CHARACTERISTICS OF THE
# BERGAMASCO

## BEHAVIOR AND TEMPERAMENT

Strong, sound and brave, the Bergamasco is, above all, very intelligent and balanced. The intelligence of the dog has been refined through natural selection. Being alone with hundreds of sheep to look after and having to sort out difficult and unexpected problems, the Bergamasco developed a great and diverse intellect. As we have seen, our dog is a flock drover; to make him suitable for this work, careful selection was applied to eliminate excessive aggression, a highly negative trait in a sheepdog.

The Bergamasco is a peace-loving dog. He appears to have an aversion for unnecessary disputes. Puppies play together without impulse towards rivalry. As no antagonism is created between them, they grow up in harmony with each other and develop strong personal links that are never broken. This relationship exists not only between brothers and sisters, and between mothers and pups, but also between all members of a group, if allowed to live freely together.

Bergamascos show great respect for each other; they avoid

Both sexes in the Bergamasco can make delightful pets. Discuss the differences between the sexes with your breeder.

irritating or provoking one another. This tranquil and reserved behavior must not be mistaken for timidity. On the contrary, they have strong, decisive characters. Their highly developed dignity makes it possible for them to live in peace and mutual respect with each other. The manner in which Bergamascos live together in a group is reflected in their relations with human beings. The Bergamasco is a friend, never a follower. He does not submit; rather, he obeys to demonstrate affection, but will not do this under duress.

A Bergamasco always needs to understand "why" he has to do something. He needs to be treated as the intelligent being he is. Only if you can make him understand "rationally" what you want of him will he comply with pleasure, but in his own way. He will never see you as a "master," but as a friend. He will never blindly execute orders. He will look at you, trying to understand what is going through your head, and, if you cannot match his level of intelligence and common sense, he will simply walk off, bored, disillusioned and maybe even offended.

The matrix of the Bergamasco's temperament, like that of his entire behavior pattern, can be found in his historical past. The relationship that existed between shepherd and Bergamasco is absolutely unique due to the particular environmental characteristics of the type of country in which the dogs evolved. When the Bergamasco and the shepherd moved their flocks across the Alpine valleys, they were brought close together as the solitude and isolation in these zones made their bond ever stronger. Because of the life they led and the work that they carried out together, the dogs became more a part of the human world than of that of the flock. In this manner, a silent dialogue took place between shepherd and dog, who always took the lead by fixing his eyes on the shepherd, ready to respond to even the slightest variation in the shepherd's expression.

With this knowledge of thousands of years' experience, today's Bergamasco is adjusting himself to life in a new environment. In fact, the human family has now become his flock. Attentive and reserved, he participates constantly in everything that goes on around him and, even when he appears to be asleep, his eyes will be following all that is happening.

The Bergamasco is a family dog in the true sense of the word. He does not select a particular individual to whom he is dedi-

## DOGS, DOGS, GOOD FOR YOUR HEART!

People usually purchase dogs for companionship, but studies show that dogs can help to improve their owners' health and level of activity, as well as lower a human's risk of coronary heart disease. Without even realizing it, when a person puts time into exercising, grooming and feeding a dog, he also puts more time into his own personal health care. Dog owners establish more routine schedules for their dogs to follow, which can have positive effects on their own health. Dogs also teach us patience, offer unconditional love and provide the joy of having a furry friend to pet!

cated; he doesn't want a "master," as is the case for many other breeds. Thanks to his great sensibility, he behaves in a slightly different manner toward each of the family members, adapting to their personal characters and acting accordingly. In this way, little by little, the Bergamasco becomes an inseparable member of your family without your really noticing it.

Although not instinctively aggressive, the Bergamasco is an excellent watchdog because he doesn't like strangers invading his world. He energetically expresses this aversion by preventing them from stepping over the boundaries of "his" property. However, when he is released from his duty of guardian, he is friendly with everybody.

Another factor in the Bergamasco's behavior pattern is his approach to the young ones of the flock, both lambs and children. He fully realizes that they are babies and reacts accordingly. A favorite

*The pet Bergamasco will adopt the children of the family as charges in his herd. Generally, Bergamascos make excellent companions for youngsters, taking on the dual role of playmate and protector.*

**DO YOU WANT TO LIVE LONGER?**
If you like to volunteer, it is wonderful if you can take your dog to a nursing home once a week for several hours. The elder community loves to have a dog with which to visit, and often your dog will bring a bit of companionship to someone who is lonely or somewhat detached from the world. You will be not only bringing happiness to someone else but also keeping your dog busy—and we haven't even mentioned the fact that it has been discovered that volunteering helps to increase your own longevity!

shepherd's tale concerns a Bergamasco who discovered a lamb abandoned by its mother. He warmed it up by licking it, and guided it back to the fold with infinite patience and perseverance. This behavior clearly demonstrates the protective instinct also common to wolves, in which not only the parents but also the whole pack collaborates in feeding, watching over and protecting the cubs. Thus, his relationship with the children of the household is something special; their presence awakens his most profound and primitive instincts, both as wolf and as sheepdog. Patient, tolerant, attentive and protective, he seeks children's company, encouraging their socialization process and development of the new puppy. Early puppy classes can be helpful with socialization and other minor puppy manners, but don't expect your Bergamasco to be obedient except on his own terms. Gentle positive reinforcement can go a long way in helping your Bergamasco decide that a bit of training is not against his grain or harmful to his independent nature. The Bergamasco must be given a reason for doing something.

games and treating them with a very particular kind of politeness and gentility. He establishes a true friendship with them. He is an excellent nanny!

## ARE YOU READY FOR A BERGAMASCO?

Living with a Bergamasco has to be seen as an enjoyable privilege, but one has to be cut out for the duty. The Bergamasco is certainly not everybody's cup of *caffé*. His appearance, his character and his wonderful gifts of sensibility and intelligence, all products of his history and breeding, have made him into a precious rarity that is not easy to understand completely.

### BERGAMASCO-STYLE OBEDIENCE

Introducing the puppy to new situations, people, children, dogs and noises are all part of the early

Equally unique in looks and personality, the Bergamasco, with his flocked coat and dignified air, commands attention in the show ring.

Repetitive commands become boring and useless for the Bergamasco, as they want to know, "Why must I do this and for what good reason?" Given its heritage, the Bergamasco is a thinking breed, able to take responsibility on its own for the flocks that were left under its care. This stable, independent thinker, who challenges our very existence in today's world, is what we have come to know and to love. Today, the Bergamasco remains the same, a highly intelligent animal that reasons rationally before reacting to a particular request.

Once the Bergamasco respects you as a partner whom he loves and trusts, then and only then will he respond to your commands (requests) with pleasure. One puppy owner commented to me that her puppy, Denali, did very well in puppy class, except refused to obey the stay command. Whenever the owner walked away from Denali, the puppy continually followed her everywhere in the class. Denali never did decide to obey the stay command.

### AN OWNER'S DESCRIPTION

Leslie Fisher tells her story: "Lampeo came to us from Italy, a gift from our son, at 11 p.m. on Christmas Eve. We picked him up at the most deserted airport. He was just nine months old and

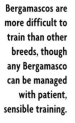

**Bergamascos are more difficult to train than other breeds, though any Bergamasco can be managed with patient, sensible training.**

only understood Italian. We had read all that was written about Bergamascos, but frankly, we didn't believe all that we read. It did not sound like they were writing about a dog. Since that December 24, we have grown into believers. Lampeo is not just a dog, but he had to teach us that.

"This is what Lampeo has taught us: He is an animal of great pride and dignity—don't shame or humiliate him. He has a long memory for offenses and will need time to rebuild his trust. Our granddaughter frightened him and it took a year for Lampeo to gain her trust again. Lampeo communicates his wants and needs. We serve him well. He likes to hug.

"He is not a dog to take to obedience school. Lampeo does exactly as we wish—on his own terms. To force him is to offend him. He will be bribed, however. Lampeo is always calm, always reserved. He barks only for a reason. We never had to train him on a leash. When on the leash he is controlled, but it must be because he chooses to be. He is a creature of great intelligence."

Once the trust has been established between you and your Bergamasco, an ongoing working partnership becomes an everyday part of life, not out of commands or orders, but out of the mutual respect, love and understanding that both of you have found.

# BREED STANDARD FOR THE

# BERGAMASCO

## THE FÉDÉRATION CYNOLOGIQUE INTERNATIONALE STANDARD FOR THE BERGAMASCO

**Origin:** Italy

**Utilization:** Shepherd dog used in driving and guarding herds.

**Classification:** Group 1 (Sheep-dogs and Cattledogs, except Swiss cattledogs); Section 1 (Sheepdogs); Without working trial.

**Brief Historical Summary:** This ancient breed of droving dogs of herds has spread all over the region of the Italian Alps; the total number of these dogs was especially great in the Bergamasco valleys, where the breeding of sheep was highly developed.

**General Appearance:** The Berga-masco Shepherd is a dog of medium size, of rustic appearance with an abundant coat covering all parts of the body, of a powerful and compact construction but very well proportioned.

**Behavior and Temperament:** The Bergamasco is a very intelligent animal, courageous but not aggressive without cause. His function is to guide and guard the herd, a task for which he shows exemplary disposition thanks to his vigilance, his concentration and psychological balance. His learning faculty and determination, combined with his moderation and patience, make him an excellent guard and companion dog, suited to the most diverse uses. He establishes a close relationship with man.

**Head:** The length of the head is four-tenths the height at the with-ers, with the skull and muzzle of equal length, parallel to one another, and joined at a pro-nounced stop. The skin on the head is tight with no wrinkles.

**Skull:** The skull is broad and slightly domed between the ears and rounded at the forehead. The skull is about as wide as it is long, and features a prominent occiput and a marked median furrow.

**Muzzle:** The depth and width of the muzzle, measured at midpoint, are each about half the length of the muzzle. The muzzle is blunt, tapering only slightly toward the nose. The lips are tight and of black pigment. The inner corner of the mouth reaches back to a vertical line drawn down from the outside corner of the eye.

**Teeth:** The jaw is wide with a full complement of strong, evenly spaced, white teeth meeting in a scissors bite. The line of the incisors is straight and perpendicular to the outside lines of the jaw.

**Nose:** The nose is large and black, with big, well-opened nostrils. In profile, the nose is on the same line as the top of the muzzle and does not extend beyond the forepart of the muzzle.

**Eyes:** The eyes are large, oval, and set just slightly obliquely. Eye color is brown, with the darkness of the color varying with the color of the coat. The eye rims are tight-fitting and black. The expression is attentive and calm.

**Ears:** Set high, semi-drooping, i.e., the last two-thirds of the lobe are drooping. When the dog is attentive, the ear lifts slightly at its base. Triangular shape. Length is between 11 and 13 cm, width 6.5 to 8 cm. The tip is slightly rounded. Hair on the ear is a little

## BERGAMASCO IN PROFILE

Two dogs in profile, both showing correct type, structure and proportion with variations on correct coat. The top dog shows wide flat cords all over except the face and tail, which are less inclined to cord. The bottom dog shows finer cords on the front half and broad flat cords over the hindquarters. Both tail carriages are correct. Color ranges from almost black (top) to light silver gray (bottom).

wavy and soft; ends up forming fringes on the tip.

**Neck:** Upper profile is slightly convex. The neck is a little bit shorter than the head. The skin is never flabby, so always without dewlap. Hair must be dense.

**Body:** The Bergamasco is very slightly longer than tall.

**Withers:** Well defined from the straight topline, high and long. The neck harmoniously joined to the body.

**Topline:** Inclines very slightly downward from prominent withers to a strong, broad back with a straight upper line. Loin is well muscled and broad. Rump wide, strong, well muscled and slightly sloping, about 30° downward from the horizontal.

**Chest:** Must be ample, brisket down to the level of the elbows

and well curved. The depth of the rib cage is equal to half the dog's height at the withers.

**Tail:** Set on last third of rump, thick and strong at its root, tapering towards its extremity. Covered with goat-like hair. When the dog is standing, it reaches the hock. At rest the tail is carried "sabre" fashion, i.e., dropping in its first third, then slightly curved in last third. In action the dog wags his tail like a flag.

**Forequarters:** Seen from front as in profile, limbs are straight. Height from ground to elbow is 50% the height at the withers.

**Shoulders:** The shoulders are massive and strong. The shoulder blade is wide and sufficiently long. Its length should not be less than a quarter of the height at the withers. Its average lay back from the horizontal should be 55°–60°.

**Upper Arm:** At the shoulder the upper arm should be strong and well muscled. Humerus is a strong bone only a little longer than the shoulder blade. The angle between shoulder blade and humerus should be about 115°.

**Elbows:** Elbows are in close proximity to the chest wall, set on a plane parallel to the body. The coat from the elbow down must be profuse, long and matted.

Head study showing correct type and proportion with the typical disheveled appearance. The coat on the head does not usually cord.

## WHAT IS A STANDARD?

According to England's Kennel Club, "The Breed Standard is the 'Blueprint' of the ideal specimen in each breed approved by a governing body, e.g. The Kennel Club, the Fédération Cynologique Internationale (FCI) and the American Kennel Club."

Preparation of standards differs from country to country, but they usually are written by or with advice from the breed club. The Kennel Club goes on to say: "Breed Standards are not changed lightly to avoid 'changing the standard to fit the current dogs' and the health and well-being of future dogs is always taken into account when new standards are prepared or existing ones altered."

**Forearm:** Forearm is strong and straight. Radius has the same length or is slightly longer than the humerus. The pastern joint (carpus) is mobile and lean with the pisiform bone clearly protruding. Pastern (metacarpus) is straight when viewed from the front, seen in profile is slightly sloping to the front.

**Foot:** Oval shaped with well closed and arched toes.

**Hindquarters:** Limbs straight, as much in profile as from behind.

**Upper Thigh:** Upper thigh is wide, strong and well muscled.

The pelvis-femoral joint angle must be about 100°.

**Lower Thigh:** The lower thigh must be strong with robust bones and lean muscles. Tibia is slightly longer than the femur and the tibia-femoral angle (stifle joint) is about 110°.

**Hock:** Hock is an essential articular muscular complex for producing the drive and should be really wide. There is a well-defined furrow between the tendon and the bone above the hock.

**Rear Pastern (Metatarsus):** When the dog is standing in balance, the metatarsal must be perpendicular to the ground and posed in such a manner that a vertical line, drawn from the point of the ischium, touches the ground just in front of the toes. It should be relatively short to permit a low, harmonious gait. The distance from the point of the hock to the ground must be about 25% of the height at the withers.

**Foot:** Rear feet are the same as the front ones except slightly smaller. Eventually dewclaws must be eliminated.

**Skin:** Tight to the body, must be fine all over, but especially on the ears and forequarters. Neck without dewlap and head without wrinkles. Color of the mucous

The adult Bergamasco coat takes up to three years to develop. The puppy will experience ever-changing coat development as he matures.

membranes and third eyelids must be black.

**Coat:** Texture typical of this breed is the presence of three types of hair: the undercoat, fine, dense and oily, adhering to the skin and forming a waterproof, protective layer; the goat hair, strong and rough as in goats and which stays smooth without tufting; and the woolly coat, finer in texture which grows together in flocks. The distribution of the various types of hair over the body is not homogeneous. In the region of the withers down to roughly half the depth of the thorax, only goat hair is present, forming a smooth saddle. In the rear section of the trunk and on the limbs, together with the goat hair that is still present there, there is a vast amount of woolly hair from which the particular masses of hair, known as "flocks," originate. The "flock" should be larger at its base, flat, irregular and sometimes opening fan-wise. This is due to the abundant presence of goat hair mixed with the woolly hair. The flocks must start from the topline of the back and fall on the sides of the body. On the head, the hair is less harsh and covers the eyes. On the limbs, the coat must be evenly distributed everywhere in the shape of soft flocks falling towards the ground, forming a kind of pilaster on the front and flocks on the hindquarters.

**Color:** The coat color is gray of all possible shades, from a most delicate gray to black. It can be solid or with black patches. An all-black coat is allowed if opaque. An all-white coat is proscribed so as all other colors. Shadings of Isabella or fawn because of the dead coat on the tip of the maps can be present. White patches are accepted as long as their surface is not more than a fifth of the total surface of the coat.

**Gait:** Because a herding dog is required to be in constant motion while the flock is being driven, correct, efficient movement is essential. The natural and preferred gait for the Bergamasco is a free, extended, elastic trot with both front and rear feet remaining close to the ground. Pasterns are supple and flex freely. When moving, the dog's head moves forward so that the head is nearly even with the back line. *Disqualification:* Ambling, when it appears to be the dog's natural gait.

**Size and Weight:** *Size*—The ideal height at the withers for males is 60 cm (23.5 in) with a tolerance of 2 cm either above or below (1 in). For the females 56 cm (22 in), also with a tolerance of 2 cm more or less. *Weight*— Males 32–38 kg (70–84 lb). Females 26–32 kg (57–71 lb).

The desired movement for the breed is a free, elastic trot with both the front and rear feet remaining close to the ground and with the head nearly in line with the back.

# BERGAMASCO

## CHOOSING YOUR PUPPY

There are countless questions a potential owner of a Bergamasco puppy might wish to ask. Perhaps the first questions should be "Can I live comfortably with this dog for the next 15 years? And am I able to give this dog a good home?" Before you acquire your new puppy, make certain that the Bergamasco is the right breed for you! Choose carefully and spend time finding the dog that best fulfills your idea of a long-time faithful companion.

A few further questions you might ask of yourself before acquiring a dog include the following: Will the puppy someday become the dog that I want? Will the puppy fit into my living environment, inside and out? Does this puppy have the personality that I am looking for? Am I interested in showing? Will this dog get along with my children? Am I looking for a lively, outgoing puppy or a calmer, quieter companion? Do I want a male or female? What differences are there between male and female dogs? Will this dog get along

### "YOU BETTER SHOP AROUND!"

Finding a reputable breeder who sells healthy pups is very important, but make sure that the breeder you choose is not only someone you respect but also someone with whom you feel comfortable. Your breeder will be a resource long after you buy your puppy, and you must be able to call with reasonable questions without being made to feel like a pest! If you don't connect on a personal level, investigate some other breeders before making a final decision.

with my other pets? Is the Bergamasco's coat difficult to tend to? Are there any innate/inherited health problems known in this breed with which I need to concern myself? Will my selected dog breeder be reliable for ongoing communication to help me as the puppy and I learn to live together? What am I expected to do as an owner of this special breed of dog? These questions are but a few to help you choose the right breed for yourself and your family.

Talk to several owners who have been involved with Bergamascos for some time, and go visit the puppies and adults so you can see the different growth stages and personality characteristics. For instance, many puppies may be very outgoing and personable, which will be initially a little easier for a family with small children to work with because the pups are readily approachable and not easily frightened. Other puppies are a bit serious or more hesitant of strangers, or appear less sure of themselves. This type of puppy initially may need a little more personal attention to make him comfortable in his new environment. This does not mean that the puppy will be less active or playful. This tranquil and reserved behavior in the puppy should not be mistaken

## DIFFERENCES BETWEEN DOGS AND BITCHES

The main difference that comes to mind when discussing the two genders is size. The female, when mature, is usually smaller in size than the male, and visually you should be able to see the more feminine facial expressions. Male and female Bergamascos show and share many similar personality characteristics and traits, depending upon the given situation and personality of each particular Bergamasco.

for insecurity; on the contrary, this puppy can be independent and knows what he wants.

Are you ready to choose your new companion? Have you decided on the sex, color and personality characteristics that you are looking for? It would be best to visit the breeder and see the sire, dam and other members of the litter's family. This will give you a general idea of what characteristics your puppy could have and how he will likely mature.

It is a great feeling to see a litter of exuberant and squirming puppies and to choose the right one for you. The breeder can be great help to you in making your

Finding and selecting a Bergamasco puppy require time and commitment, as does dog ownership. When you find the puppy that suits you, you will know it for certain.

## TEMPERAMENT COUNTS

Your selection of a good puppy can be determined by your needs. A show potential or a good pet? It is your choice. Every puppy, however, should be of good temperament. Although show-quality puppies are bred and raised with emphasis on physical conformation, responsible breeders strive for equally good temperament. Do not buy from a breeder who concentrates solely on physical beauty at the expense of personality.

decision and in choosing the puppy best suited to your personality and lifestyle.

A puppy represents the breeder's knowledge and reputation. A lot of love, time and thought went into your new companion; each and every puppy that leaves the breeder is a love lost and hopefully a new friend gained. Acquiring a new puppy should be taken seriously; it is a meaningful commitment that will last for the dog's lifetime.

Your puppy should have a health certificate from a certified veterinarian, as well as all of the necessary vaccinations for a puppy of his age. A three- to

**YOUR SCHEDULE . . .**
If you lead an erratic, unpredictable life, with daily or weekly changes in your work requirements, consider the problems of owning a puppy. The new puppy has to be fed regularly, socialized (loved, petted, handled, introduced to other people) and, most importantly, allowed to go outdoors for house-training. As the dog gets older, he can be more tolerant of deviations in his feeding and relief schedule.

four-generation pedigree, as well as the registration papers from the appropriate kennel club of the country in which you reside, should be given to you. In the US, there are a few clubs to consider, since the Bergamasco is not recognized by the country's leading registry, the American Kennel Club (AKC). ARBA, the States Kennel Club and the United Kennel Club do recognize the breed. In Britain, The Kennel Club is the main registering body in the country. With whom you register your dog will vary from country to country since there could be more than one club that accepts registration of the breed.

Once you have decided that the Bergamasco is the right companion for you, be prepared to bring the puppy home between 12 to 14 weeks of age.

Your Bergamasco pup should appear alert, active and healthy. The breeder should be able to answer all of your questions about helping the pup settle into his new home.

Usually 6 to 8 puppies have been whelped, and it is not advisable that the puppy be taken away any earlier since there is so much that the puppy learns from his siblings and mother. The pups bond now and forever with their mother and siblings. They learn socialization and posturing within the pack,

### PEDIGREE VS. REGISTRATION CERTIFICATE

Too often new owners are confused between these two important documents. Your puppy's pedigree, essentially a family tree, is a written record of a dog's genealogy of three generations or more. The pedigree will show you the names as well as performance titles of all dogs in your pup's background. Your breeder must provide you with a registration application, with his part properly filled out. You must complete the application and send it to the registering organization with the proper fee.

The seller must provide you with complete records to identify the puppy. The seller should provide the buyer with the following: breed; sex, color and markings; date of birth; litter number (when available); names and registration numbers of the parents; breeder's name; and date sold or delivered.

so puppy play is invaluable for this. Appropriate behavior and respect are taught by the mother to her young, making a lifelong impact on the Bergamasco. Due to this closely guided upbringing, Bergamascos are usually secure within themselves, well socialized and ready to take on new adventures with their new families, whether in the form of herding sheep or playing with children.

## PREPARING PUPPY'S PLACE IN YOUR HOME

Researching your breed and finding a breeder are only two aspects of the "homework" you will have to do before taking your Bergamasco puppy home. You will also have to prepare your home and family for the new addition. Much as you would prepare a nursery for a newborn baby, you will need to designate a place in your home that will be the puppy's own. How you prepare your home will depend on how much freedom the dog will be allowed. Whatever you decide, you must ensure that he has a place that he can "call his own."

When you bring your new puppy into your home, you are bringing him into what will become his home as well. Obviously, you did not buy a puppy with the intentions of catering to his every whim and allowing him to "rule the roost," but in order for a puppy to grow into a stable, well-adjusted dog, he has to feel comfortable in his surroundings. Remember, he is leaving the warmth and security of his mother and littermates, as well as the familiarity of the only place he has ever known, so it is important to make his transition as easy as possible. By preparing a place in your home for the puppy, you are making him feel as welcome as possible

### INHERIT THE MIND

In order to know whether or not a puppy will fit into your lifestyle, you need to assess his personality. A good way to do this is to interact with his parents. Your pup inherits not only his appearance but also his personality and temperament from the sire and dam. If the parents are fearful or overly aggressive, these same traits may likely show up in your puppy.

in a strange new place. It should not take him long to get used to it, but the sudden shock of being transplanted is somewhat traumatic for a young pup. Imagine how a small child would feel in the same situation—that is how your puppy must be feeling. It is up to you to reassure him and to

Although sharing a long history with sheep, the Bergamasco is a peaceful, friendly breed that should welcome introductions to new acquaintances of all kinds.

training. For example, crate training is a popular and successful house-training method. In addition, a crate can keep your dog safe during travel and, perhaps most importantly, a crate provides your dog with a place of his own in your home. It serves as a "doggie bedroom" of sorts—your Bergamasco can curl up in his crate when he wants to sleep or when he just

let him know, "Little *cane*, you are going to like it here!"

## WHAT YOU SHOULD BUY

### CRATE

To someone unfamiliar with the use of crates in dog training, it may seem like punishment to shut a dog in a crate, but this is not the case at all. Although all breeders do not advocate crate training, more and more breeders and trainers around the world are recommending crates as preferred tools for show puppies and pet puppies alike.

Crates are not cruel—crates have many humane and highly effective uses in dog care and

### ARE YOU PREPARED?

Unfortunately, when a puppy is bought by someone who does not take into consideration the time and attention that dog ownership requires, it is the puppy who suffers when he is either abandoned or placed in a shelter by a frustrated owner. So all of the "homework" you do in preparation for your pup's arrival will benefit you both. The more informed you are, the more you will know what to expect and the better equipped you will be to handle the ups and downs of raising a puppy. Hopefully, everyone in the household is willing to do his part in raising and caring for the pup. The anticipation of owning a dog often brings a lot of promises from excited family members: "I will walk him every day," "I will feed him," "I will house-train him," etc., but these things take time and effort, and promises can easily be forgotten once the novelty of the new pet has worn off.

needs a break. Many dogs sleep in their crates overnight. With soft bedding and his favorite toy, a crate becomes a cozy pseudo-den for your dog. Like his ancestors, he too will seek out the comfort and retreat of a den—you just happen to be providing him with something a little more luxurious than what his early ancestors enjoyed.

As far as purchasing a crate, the type that you buy is up to you. It will most likely be one of the two most popular types: wire or fiberglass. There are advantages and disadvantages to each type. For example, a wire crate is more open, allowing the air to flow through and affording the dog a view of what is going on around him, while a fiberglass crate is sturdier. Both can double as travel crates, providing protection for the dog in the car.

The size of the crate is another thing to consider. Puppies do not stay puppies forever—in fact, sometimes it seems as if they grow right before your eyes. A small crate may be fine for a very young Bergamasco pup, but it will not do him much good for long! Unless you have the money and the inclination to buy a new crate every time your pup has a growth spurt, it is better to get one that will accommodate your dog both as a pup and at full

size. A large crate will be necessary for a fully-grown Bergamasco, who can stand around 60 cm (23.5 in) at the shoulder.

## PUPPY PERSONALITY

When a litter becomes available to you, choosing a pup out of all those adorable faces will not be an easy task! Sound temperament is of utmost importance, but each pup has its own personality and some may be better suited to you than others. A feisty, independent pup will do well in a home with older children and adults, while quiet, shy puppies will thrive in homes with minimal noise and distractions. Your breeder knows the pups best and should be able to guide you in the right direction.

PHOTO COURTESY OF DOSKOCIL

Your local pet shop should have a wide array of dog crates. Get one large enough for a full-grown Bergamasco.

Although your pup is far removed from his den-making ancestors, the denning instinct is still a part of his genetic makeup. Second, until you take your pup home, he has been sleeping amid the warmth of his mother and littermates, and while a blanket is not the same as a warm, breathing body, it still provides heat and something with which to snuggle. You will want to wash your pup's bedding frequently in case he has a toileting "accident" in his crate, and replace any blanket or padding that becomes ragged and starts to fall apart.

## CRATE-TRAINING TIPS

During crate training, you should partition off the section of the crate in which the pup stays. If he is given too big an area, this will hinder your training efforts. Crate training is based on the fact that a dog does not like to soil his sleeping quarters, so it is ineffective to keep a pup in an area that is so big that he can eliminate in one end and get far enough away from it to sleep. Also, you want to make the crate den-like for the pup. Blankets and a favorite toy will make the crate cozy for the small pup; as he grows, you may want to evict some of his "roommates" to make more room. It will take some coaxing at first, but be patient. Given some time to get used to it, your pup will adapt to his new home-within-a-home quite nicely.

### BEDDING

A nice soft crate mat in the dog's crate will help the dog feel more at home, and you may also like to give him a small blanket. First, this will take the place of the leaves, twigs, etc., that the pup would use in the wild to make a den; the pup can make his own "burrow" in the crate.

## Toys

Toys are a must for dogs of all ages, especially for curious playful pups. Puppies are the "children" of the dog world, and what child does not love toys? Chew toys provide enjoyment for both dog and owner—your dog will enjoy playing with his favorite toys, while you will enjoy the fact that they distract him from chewing on your expensive shoes and leather sofa. Puppies love to chew; in fact, chewing is a physical need for pups as they are teething, and everything looks appetizing! The full range of your possessions—from dish rag to Oriental carpet—are fair game in the eyes of a teething pup. Puppies are not all that discerning when it comes to finding something literally to "sink their teeth into"—everything tastes great!

Bergamascos are fairly aggressive chewers and only the strongest, most chew-resistant toys should be offered to them. Breeders advise owners to resist stuffed toys, because they can become de-stuffed in no time. The excited pup may ingest the stuffing, which could make him sick or cause him to choke.

Similarly, squeaky toys are quite popular, but must be avoided for the Bergamasco. Perhaps a squeaky toy can be used as an aid in training, but not for free play. If a pup "disembowels" one of these, the small plastic squeaker inside can be dangerous if swallowed. Monitor the condition of all your pup's toys carefully and get

**PUPPY APPEARANCE**
Your puppy should have a well-fed appearance but not a distended abdomen, which may indicate worms or incorrect feeding, or both. The body should be firm, with a solid feel. The skin of the abdomen should be pale pink and clean, without signs of scratching or rash. Check the hind legs to see if the dewclaws have yet been removed; the standard states that eventually they must be.

## MENTAL AND DENTAL

Toys not only help your puppy get the physical and mental stimulation he needs but also provide a great way to keep his teeth clean. Hard rubber or nylon toys, especially those constructed with grooves, are designed to scrape away plaque, preventing bad breath and gum infection.

Your local pet shop should have a wide array of leads from which you can choose one that best suits your Bergamasco.

rid of any that have been chewed to the point of becoming potentially dangerous.

Be careful of natural bones, which have a tendency to splinter into sharp, dangerous pieces. Also be careful of rawhide, which can turn into pieces that are easy to swallow, as well as become a mushy mess on your carpet.

## LEAD

A nylon lead is probably the best option, as it is the most resistant to puppy teeth should your pup take a liking to chewing on his lead. Of course, this is a habit that should be nipped in the bud, but, if your pup likes to chew on his lead, he has a very slim chance of being able to chew through the strong nylon. Nylon leads are also lightweight, which is good for a young Bergamasco who is just getting used to the idea of walking on a lead. For everyday walking and safety purposes, the nylon lead is a good choice. As your pup grows up and gets used to walking on the lead, you may want to purchase a flexible lead. These

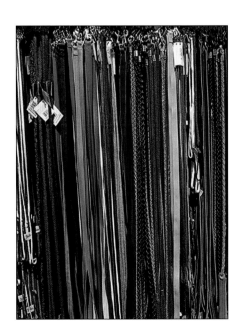

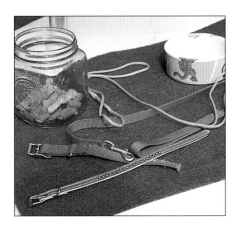

leads allow you to extend the length to give the dog a broader area to explore or to shorten the length to keep the dog near you. Flexible leads have weight limitations, so be sure to choose a lead appropriate to your Bergamasco's size.

### COLLAR

Your pup should get used to wearing a collar all the time since you will want to attach his ID tags to it; plus, you have to attach the lead to something! A lightweight nylon collar is a good choice. Make certain that the collar fits snugly enough so that the pup cannot wriggle out of it, but is loose enough so that it will not be uncomfortably tight around the pup's neck. You should be able to fit a finger or two between the pup's neck and the collar. It may take some time for your pup to get used to wearing the collar, but soon he will

## TOYS, TOYS, TOYS!

With a big variety of dog toys available, and so many that look like they would be a lot of fun for a dog, be careful in your selection. It is amazing what a set of puppy teeth can do to an innocent-looking toy, so, obviously, safety is a major consideration. Be sure to choose the most durable products that you can find. Hard nylon bones and toys are a safe bet, and many of them are offered in different scents and flavors that will be sure to capture your dog's attention. It is always fun to play a game of fetch with your dog, and there are balls and flying discs that are specially made to withstand dog teeth.

Along with your new puppy comes the need for puppy supplies. Have the necessities on hand before your puppy comes home.

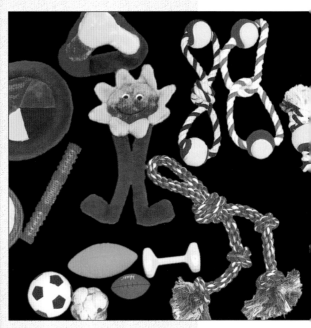

Your local pet shop sells many different kinds of food and water bowls suitable for your Bergamasco.

PHOTO COURTESY OF MIKKI PET PRODUCTS.

not even notice that it is there. Choke collars are popular for training many breeds of dog, but these are not appropriate for use on coated breeds like the Bergamasco.

### FOOD AND WATER BOWLS
Your pup will need two bowls, one for food and one for water. You may want two sets of bowls, one for indoors and one for outdoors, depending on where the dog will be fed and where he will be spending time. Stainless steel or sturdy plastic bowls are popular choices. Plastic bowls are more chewable, but dogs tend not to chew on the steel variety, which can be sterilized. It is important to buy sturdy bowls since anything is in danger of being chewed by puppy teeth and you do not want your dog to be constantly chewing apart his bowl (for his safety and for your purse!).

### CLEANING SUPPLIES
Until a pup is house-trained, you will be doing a lot of cleaning. "Accidents" will occur, which is acceptable in the beginning stages of toilet training because the puppy does not know any better. All you can do is be prepared to clean up any accidents as soon as they happen. Old rags, towels, newspapers and a safe disinfectant are good to have on hand.

# CHOOSE AN APPROPRIATE COLLAR

The **BUCKLE COLLAR** is the standard collar used for everyday purposes. Be sure that you adjust the buckle on growing puppies. Check it every day. It can become too tight overnight! These collars can be made of leather or nylon. Attach your dog's identification tags to this collar.

The **CHOKE COLLAR** is designed for training. It is constructed of highly polished steel so that it slides easily through the stainless steel loop. The idea is that the dog controls the pressure around his neck and he will stop pulling if the collar becomes uncomfortable. The Bergamasco's abundant coat makes this type of collar unsuitable.

The **HALTER** is for a trained dog that has to be restrained to prevent running away, chasing a cat and the like. Considered the most humane of all collars, it is frequently used on smaller dogs on which collars are not comfortable.

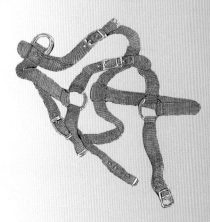

**FINANCIAL RESPONSIBILITY**
Grooming tools, collars, leashes, a crate, a dog bed and, of course, toys will be expenses to you when you first obtain your pup, and the cost will continue throughout your dog's lifetime. If your puppy damages or destroys your possessions (as most puppies surely will!) or something belonging to a neighbor, you can calculate additional expense. There is also flea and pest control, which every dog owner faces more than once. You must be able to handle the financial responsibility of owning a dog.

### BEYOND THE BASICS

The items previously discussed are the bare necessities. You will find out what else you need as you go along—grooming supplies, flea/tick protection, baby gates to partition a room, etc. These things will vary depending on your situation, but it is important that you have everything you need to feed and make your Bergamasco comfortable in his first few days at home.

### PUPPY-PROOFING YOUR HOME

Aside from making sure that your Bergamasco will be comfortable in your home, you also have to make sure that your home is safe for your

Bergamasco. This means taking precautions that your pup will not get into anything he should not get into and that there is nothing within his reach that may harm him should he sniff it, chew it, inspect it, etc. This probably seems obvious since, while you are primarily concerned with your pup's safety, at the same time you do not want your belongings to be ruined. Breakables should be placed out of reach if your dog is to have full run of the house. If he is to be limited to certain places within the house, keep any potentially dangerous items in the "off-limits" areas.

An electrical cord can pose a danger should the puppy decide to taste it—and who is going to convince a pup that it would not make a great chew toy? Cords should be fastened tightly against the wall. If your dog is going to spend time in a crate, make sure that there is nothing near his crate that he can reach if he sticks his curious little nose or paws through the openings. Just as you would with a child, keep all household cleaners and chemicals where the pup cannot reach them; antifreeze is especially dangerous to dogs.

It is also important to make sure that the outside of your home is safe. Of course, your puppy should never be unsupervised, but a pup let loose in the

## NATURAL TOXINS

Examine your grass and landscaping before bringing your puppy home. Many varieties of plants have leaves, stems or flowers that are toxic if ingested, and you can depend on a curious puppy to investigate them. Ask your vet for information on poisonous plants or research them at your library.

If you see your dog carrying a piece of vegetation in his mouth, approach him in a quiet, disinterested manner, avoid eye contact, pet him and gradually remove the plant from his mouth. Alternatively, offer him a treat and maybe he'll drop the plant on his own accord. Be sure no toxic plants are growing in your own yard or kept in your home.

It is your responsibility to clean up after your dog has relieved himself. Pet shops have various aids to assist in the clean-up job.

yard will want to run and explore, and he should be granted that freedom. Do not let a fence give you a false sense of security; you would be surprised at how crafty (and persistent) a dog can be in working out how to dig under and squeeze his way through small holes, or to jump or climb over a fence. The remedy is to make the fence well embedded into the ground and high enough so that it really is impossible for your dog to get over it (about 6 feet should suffice). Be sure to secure any gaps in the fence. Check the fence periodically to ensure that it is in good shape and make repairs as needed; a very deter-mined pup may return to the same spot to "work on it" until he is able to get through.

does not have any problems that are not apparent to you. The veterinarian will also set up a schedule for the pup's vaccinations; the breeder will inform you of which ones the pup has already received and the vet can continue from there.

## INTRODUCTION TO THE FAMILY

Bringing such a unique dog as the Bergamasco home will be momentous for the entire household, indeed the whole neighborhood! It is wise to make the introductions as low-key as possible. Bergamasco puppies may be a bit aloof and cautious of strangers. This is their nature, so do not overwhelm the puppy by having a party or parade at

*The most outgoing pup or one who is more easygoing? The breeder can help you pick a puppy whose personality will suit your family situation, lifestyle and living environment.*

## FIRST TRIP TO THE VET

You have selected your puppy, and your home and family are ready. Now all you have to do is collect your Bergamasco from the breeder and the fun begins—right? Well...not so fast. Something else you need to plan is your pup's first trip to the veterinarian. Perhaps the breeder can recommend a qualified vet who might specialize in coated breeds or herding dogs. You should have an appointment arranged for your pup before you pick him up.

The pup's first visit will consist of an overall examination to make sure that the pup

### HOW VACCINES WORK

If you've just bought a puppy, you surely know the importance of having your pup vaccinated, but do you understand how vaccines work? Vaccines contain the same bacteria or viruses that cause the disease you want to prevent, but they have been chemically modified so that they don't cause any harm. Instead, the vaccine causes your dog to produce antibodies that fight the harmful bacteria. Thus, if your dog is exposed to the disease in the future, the antibodies will destroy the viruses or bacteria.

**FEEDING TIPS**

You will probably start feeding your pup the same food that he has been getting from the breeder; the breeder should give you a few days' supply to start you off. Although you should not give your pup too many treats, you will want to have puppy treats on hand for coaxing, training, rewards, etc. Be careful, though, as a small pup's calorie requirements are relatively low and a few treats can add up to almost a full day's worth of calories without the required nutrition.

while. Gradually, each person should spend some time with the pup, one at a time, crouching down to get as close to the pup's level as possible while letting him sniff each person's hands and petting him gently. He definitely needs human attention and he needs to be touched—this is how to form an immediate bond. Just remember that the pup is experiencing many things for the first time, at the same time. There are new people, new noises, new smells and new things to investigate, so be gentle, be affectionate and be as comforting as you can be.

**PUP'S FIRST NIGHT HOME**

You have traveled home with your new charge safely in his crate. He's been to the vet for a thorough check-up; he's been

his arrival. He is apprehensive already. It is the first time he has been separated from his mother and the breeder, and the ride to your home is likely to be the first time he has been in a car. The last thing you want to do is smother him, as this will only frighten him further. This is not to say that human contact is not extremely necessary at this stage, because this is the time when a connection between the pup and his human family is formed. Gentle petting and soothing words should help console him, as well as just putting him down and letting him explore on his own (under your watchful eye, of course).

The pup may approach the family members or may busy himself with exploring for a

Give your puppy a chance to explore his new terrain under your careful watch. The active Bergamasco will welcome a fenced yard in which to play and exercise.

Your Bergamasco will surely become your child's best friend. Be sure to teach your child how to handle the dog so that it will be a mutual friendship based on respect and considerate treatment.

weighed, his papers have been examined and perhaps he's even been vaccinated and wormed as well. He's met the whole family, including the excited children and the less-than-happy cat. He's explored his area, his new bed, the yard and anywhere else he's been permitted. He's eaten his first meal at home and relieved himself in the proper place. He's heard lots of new sounds, smelled new friends and seen more of the outside world than ever before…and that was just the first day! He's worn out and is ready for bed…or so you think!

It's puppy's first night home and you are ready to say "Good night." Keep in mind that this is his first night ever to be sleeping alone. His dam and littermates are no longer at paw's length and he's a bit scared, cold and lonely. Be reassuring to your new family member, but this is not the time to spoil him and give in to his inevitable whining.

Puppies whine. They whine to let others know where they are and hopefully to get company out of it. Place your pup in his new bed or crate in his designated area and close the door. Mercifully, he may fall asleep without a peep. When the inevitable occurs, however, ignore the whining—he is fine. Be strong and keep his best inter-est in mind. Do not allow your-self to feel guilty and visit the

**IN DUE TIME**
It will take at least two weeks for your puppy to become accustomed to his new surroundings. Give him lots of love, attention, handling, frequent opportunities to relieve himself, a diet he likes to eat and a place he can call his own.

pup. Your puppy will fall asleep eventually.

Many breeders recommend placing a piece of bedding from the pup's former home in his new bed so that he recognizes and is comforted by the scent of his littermates. Others still advise placing a hot water bottle in the bed for warmth. The latter may be a good idea provided the pup doesn't attempt to suckle—he'll get good and wet, and may not fall asleep so fast.

Puppy's first night can be somewhat stressful for both the pup and his new family. Remember that you are setting the tone of nighttime at your house. Unless you want to play with your pup every night at 10 p.m., midnight and 2 a.m., don't initiate the habit. Your family will thank you, and soon so will your pup!

## PREVENTING PUPPY PROBLEMS

### SOCIALIZATION

Now that you have done all of the preparatory work and have helped your pup get accustomed to his new home and family, it is about time for you to have some fun! Socializing your Bergamasco pup gives you the opportunity to show off your new friend, and your pup gets to reap the benefits of being an adorable and intriguing creature that people will want to pet and, in general, think is absolutely precious!

Besides getting to know his new family, your puppy should be exposed to other people, animals and situations. This will help him become well adjusted as he grows up and less prone to being timid or fearful of the new

*Stress can affect dogs, too. A Bergamasco's growing-up years should be happy and stress-free.*

things he will encounter. Of course, he must not come into close contact with dogs you don't know well until his course of injections is fully complete.

Your pup's socialization began with the breeder, but now it is your responsibility to continue it. The socialization he receives until the age of 16 weeks is the most critical, as this is the time when he forms his impressions of the outside world. The breeder is especially careful during the eight-to-ten-week-old period, also known as the fear period. The interaction the pup receives during this time should be gentle and reassuring. Lack of socialization, and/or negative experiences during the socialization period, can manifest itself in fear and aggression as the dog grows up. Your puppy needs lots of positive interaction, which of course

includes human contact, affection, handling and exposure to other animals.

Once your pup has received his necessary vaccinations, feel free to take him out and about (on his lead, of course). Walk him around the neighborhood, take him on your daily errands, let people pet him, let him meet other dogs and pets, etc. Puppies do not have to try to make friends; there will be no shortage of people who will want to introduce themselves. Just make sure that you carefully supervise each meeting. If the neighborhood children want to say hello, for example, that is great—children and pups most often make great companions. However, sometimes an excited child can unintentionally handle a pup too roughly, or an overzealous pup can playfully nip a little too hard. You want to make socialization experiences positive ones. What a pup learns during this very formative stage will affect his attitude toward future encounters. You want your dog to be comfortable around everyone. A pup that has a bad experience with a child may grow up to be a dog that is shy around or aggressive toward children.

### CONSISTENCY IN TRAINING

Dogs, being pack animals, naturally need a leader, or else they try to establish dominance in

**MANNERS MATTER**
During the socialization process, a puppy should meet people, experience different environments and definitely be exposed to other canines. Through playing and interacting with other dogs, your puppy will learn lessons, ranging from controlling the pressure of his jaws by biting his littermates to the inner-workings of the canine pack that he will apply to his human relationships for the rest of his life. That is why removing a puppy from the litter too early can be detrimental to the pup's development.

their packs. When you welcome a dog into your family, the choice of who becomes the leader and who becomes the "pack" is entirely up to you! Your pup's intuitive quest for dominance and the sheer irre-

### PUP MEETS WORLD

Thorough socialization includes not only meeting new people but also being introduced to new experiences such as riding in the car, having his coat brushed, hearing the television, walking in a crowd—the list is endless. The more your pup experiences, and the more positive the experiences are, the less of a shock and the less frightening it will be for your pup to encounter new things.

sistibility of a Bergamasco puppy give the pup almost an unfair advantage in getting the upper hand!

A pup will definitely test the waters to see what he can and cannot do. Do not give in to those pleading eyes—stand your ground when it comes to disciplining the pup and make sure that all family members do the

same. It will only confuse the pup if Mother tells him to get off the sofa when he is used to sitting up there with Father to watch the nightly news. Avoid discrepancies by having all members of the household decide on the rules before the pup even comes home...and be consistent in enforcing them! Early training shapes the dog's personality, so you cannot be unclear in what you expect.

## COMMON PUPPY PROBLEMS

The best way to prevent puppy problems is to be proactive in stopping an undesirable behavior as soon as it starts. The old saying "You can't teach an old dog new tricks" does not necessarily hold true, but it *is* true that it is much easier to discourage bad behavior in a young developing pup than to wait until the pup's bad behavior becomes the adult dog's bad habit. There are some problems that are especially prevalent in puppies as they develop.

### NIPPING

As puppies start to teethe, they feel the need to sink their teeth into anything available...unfortunately, that usually includes your fingers, arms, hair and toes. You may find this behavior cute for the first five seconds...until you feel just how sharp those puppy teeth are. Nipping is something you want to discourage immediately and consistently with a firm "No!" (or whatever number of firm "Nos" it takes for him to understand that you mean business). Then, replace your finger with an appropriate chew toy. While this behavior is merely annoying when the dog is young, it can become dangerous as your Bergamasco's adult teeth grow in and his jaws develop, and he continues to think it is okay to nibble on his human friends. Your Bergamasco does not mean any harm with a friendly nip, but he also does not know his own strength.

### CRYING/WHINING

Your pup will often cry, whine, whimper, howl or make some type of commotion when he is left alone. This is basically his way of calling out for attention to make sure that you know he is there and that you have not forgotten about him. Your puppy feels insecure when he is left alone, when you are out of the house and he is in his crate or when you are in another part of the house and he cannot see you. The noise he is making is an expression of the anxiety he feels at being alone, so he needs to be taught that being alone is okay. You are not actually training the dog to stop making noise; rather, you are training

**CHEWING TIPS**

Chewing goes hand in hand with nipping in the sense that a teething puppy is always looking for a way to soothe his aching gums. In this case, instead of chewing on you, he may have taken a liking to your favorite shoe or something else that he should not be chewing. Again, realize that this is a normal canine behavior that does not need to be discouraged, only redirected. Your pup just needs to be taught what is acceptable to chew on and what is off-limits. Consistently tell him "No!" when you catch him chewing on something forbidden and give him a chew toy.

Conversely, praise him when you catch him chewing on something appropriate. In this way, you are discouraging the inappropriate behavior and reinforcing the desired behavior. The puppy's chewing should stop after his adult teeth have come in, but an adult dog continues to chew for various reasons—perhaps because he is bored, needs to relieve tension or just likes to chew. That is why it is important to redirect his chewing when he is still young.

him to feel comfortable when he is alone and thus removing the need for him to make the noise.

This is where the crate with cozy bedding and a toy comes in handy. You want to know that your pup is safe when you are not there to supervise, and you know that he will be safe in his crate rather than roaming freely about the house. In order for the pup to stay in his crate without making a fuss, he first needs to be comfortable in his crate. On that note, it is extremely important that the crate is never used as a form of punishment; this will cause the pup to view the crate as a negative place, rather than as a place of his own for safety and retreat.

Accustom the pup to the crate in short, gradually increas-ing time intervals in which you put him in the crate, maybe with a treat, and stay in the room with him. If he cries or makes a fuss, do not go to him, but stay in his sight. Gradually he will realize that staying in his crate is just fine without your help, and it will not be so traumatic for him when you are not around. You may want to leave the radio on softly when you leave the house; the sound of human voices may be comforting to him.

Be reassuring and gentle when dealing with a puppy so that he does not come to distrust the outside world.

A well-cared-for Bergamasco pup is a happy and confident one.

## DIETARY AND FEEDING CONSIDERATIONS

### GETTING STARTED

When you take your Bergamasco home, your breeder will give you feeding instructions for the new puppy. The breeder will recommend a specific puppy food to help maintain the proper nutrition and growth rate. After 6 months and until 12 months of age, a Bergamasco should only be given a low-protein meat-based food, twice a day. After he is a year old, feeding once a day is sufficient.

It is important to be very consistent when feeding your puppy. Your puppy should eat at the same time and place every day. Once feeding time is over, any leftover food should be discarded. Never leave the food out all day. Your puppy must learn to eat at the appropriate times; otherwise, you will never know when or how much your puppy consumes in a given day. Teaching your puppy good eating habits from the beginning of his young life will lead to a mature, healthy and polite adult.

### NUTRITION

Historically, the Bergamasco relied on relatively small quantities of food. Their diets consisted primarily of milk and cheese products, and they hunted for

### STORING DOG FOOD

You must store your dry dog food carefully. Open packages of dog food quickly lose their vitamin value, usually within 90 days of being opened. Mold spores and vermin could also contaminate the food.

meat as well. They were always recognized as thin, medium-sized dogs that worked with the flocks.

Today, their basic needs have not changed much, as a full diet of cereal was never a part of the carnivore heritage. Whole basic protein was the sustenance that enabled the dogs to work throughout the day. Their method of survival provided them with relatively low overall amounts of protein, which has become an important factor in their diet today. The Bergamasco can have a problem with the high percentage of protein in today's convenience foods. It is important to note that not all protein foods are the same. The higher the biological value, the more useful the protein is to the dog and the less quantity the dog needs to sustain himself nutritionally.

For example, meat (muscle-meat), fish and dairy products are complete proteins needed nutritionally to help in daily bodily functions, including the maintenance of the skin and coat. A cereal-only diet is less complete in providing essential levels of high-quality protein, minerals, enzymes and fatty acids. In today's measurements, the optimum protein level for the Bergamasco is provided by a whole-meat diet with a protein level of between 8–15%. Some grain products, mixed in with the whole-meat meals, should

## FOOD PREFERENCE

If you choose to feed a commercially prepared dog food, you will have to choose wisely. There is no majority consensus among veterinary scientists as to the value of nutrient analysis (protein, fat, fiber, moisture, ash, cholesterol, minerals, etc.). All agree that feeding trials are what matter most, but you also have to consider the individual dog. The dog's weight, age and activity level, and what pleases his taste, all must be considered. It is probably best to take the advice of your veterinarian. Every dog has individual dietary requirements, and should be fed accordingly.

If your dog is fed a complete, balanced dog food, he does not require supplements of meat or vegetables. Dogs do appreciate a little variety in their diets, so you may choose to stay with the same brand but vary the flavor. Alternatively, you may wish to add a little flavored stock to give a difference to the taste.

**FEEDING TIPS**

- Dog food must be served at room temperature, neither too hot nor too cold. Fresh water, changed often and served in a clean bowl, is mandatory, especially when feeding dry food.
- Never feed your dog from the table while you are eating, and never feed your dog leftovers from your own meal. They usually contain too much fat and too much seasoning. Certain "people foods," such as chocolate and onions, are actually toxic to dogs.
- Dogs must chew their food. Hard pellets are excellent; soups and stews are to be avoided.
- Don't add leftovers or any extras to commercial dog food. Dog food is usually balanced, and adding something extra destroys the balance.
- Except for age-related changes, dogs do not require dietary variations. They can be fed the same diet, day after day, without their becoming bored or ill.

### KINDS OF FOODS FOR YOUR DOG

Today the choices of food for your Bergamasco are many and varied if you choose to feed a manufactured dog food. There are dozens of brands of food in all sorts of flavors and textures, ranging from puppy diets to those for seniors. There are even hypoallergenic and low-calorie diets available. Because your Bergamasco's food has a bearing on coat, health and temperament, and because the Bergamasco has special lower-protein diet requirements, it is essential that the most suitable diet is selected for a Bergamasco of his age. It is fair to say, however, that even experienced owners can be perplexed by the enormous range of foods available. Only understanding what is best for your dog will help you reach an informed decision.

Dog foods are produced in three basic types: dry, semi-moist and canned. Dry foods are useful for the cost-conscious, for overall they tend to be less expensive than semi-moist or canned foods. Dry foods also contain the least fat and the most preservatives. In general, canned foods are made up of 60–70% water, while semi-moist ones often contain so much sugar that they are perhaps the least preferred by owners, even though their dogs seem to like them.

When selecting your dog's diet, three stages of development

complete the food and help to metabolize the protein properly. Too high a percentage of protein in the Bergamasco's diet can help to cause obsessive scratching, which can cause other skin problems as well. Keep in mind that the Bergamasco is a carnivore and therefore needs to have his true nutritional requirements met to keep him functioning properly.

## "DOES THIS COLLAR MAKE ME LOOK FAT?"

While humans may obsess about how trim their bodies are, many people believe that extra weight on their dogs is a good thing. The truth is, pets should not be over- or under-weight, as both can lead to or signal sickness. Extra weight, as well as weight loss, can be hard to detect under the Bergamasco's abundant coat. In order to tell how fit your pet is, run your hands over his ribs. Are his ribs buried under a layer of fat or are they sticking out considerably? If your pet is within his normal weight range, you should be able to feel the ribs easily, but they should not protrude abnormally. Some breeds do tend to be leaner while some are a bit stockier, but making sure your dog is the right weight for his breed will certainly contribute to his good health.

must be considered: the puppy stage, the adult stage and the senior stage.

### PUPPY STAGE

Puppies instinctively want to suck milk from their mother's teats; a normal puppy will exhibit this behavior just a few moments following birth. If puppies do not attempt to suckle within the first half-hour or so, they should be encouraged to do so by placing them on the nipples, having

selected ones with plenty of milk. This early milk supply is important in providing the essential colostrum, which protects the puppies during the first eight to ten weeks of their lives. A mother's milk is much better than any milk formula, despite there being some excellent ones available. If the puppies do not feed, the breeder will have to feed them by hand. For those with less experience, advice from a veterinarian is important so that not only the right quantity of milk is fed but also that of correct quality, fed at suitably frequent intervals, usually every two hours during the first few days of life.

Puppies should be allowed to nurse from their mothers for about the first six weeks, although, starting around the third or fourth week, the breeder will begin to introduce small portions of suitable solid food. Most breeders like to introduce

**Puppies are usually weaned from their dam by the time they are seven to eight weeks of age. These pups are eating solid food together at the feeding tray.**

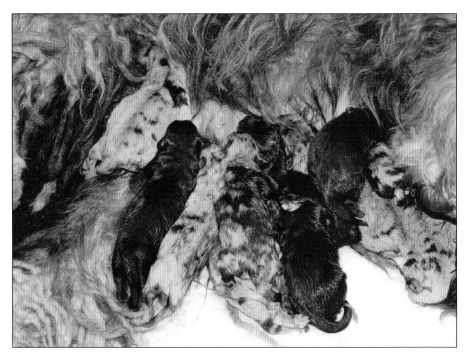

alternate milk and meat meals initially, building up to weaning time.

By the time the puppies are seven or a maximum of eight weeks old, they should be fully weaned and fed solely on a proprietary puppy food. Selection of the most suitable, good-quality diet at this time is essential, for a puppy's fastest growth rate is during the first year of life. Vets are usually able to offer advice in this regard and, although the frequency of meals will be reduced over time, only when a young dog has reached the age of about 12 months should an adult diet be fed to him.

Puppy and junior diets should be well balanced for the needs of your dog so that, except in certain circumstances, additional vitamins, minerals and proteins will not be required.

### ADULT DIETS

A dog is considered an adult when he has stopped growing, so in general the diet of a Bergamasco can be changed to an adult one at about 12 months of age. Again you should rely upon your veterinarian or breeder to recommend an acceptable maintenance diet. Major dog-food manufacturers specialize in this type of food, and it is merely necessary for you to select one that is suitable for the Bergamasco and that is most appropriate for your dog's individual needs. Active dogs may have different requirements than sedate dogs.

### SENIOR DIETS

As dogs get older, their metabolism changes. The older dog usually exercises less, moves more slowly and sleeps more. This change in lifestyle and physiological performance requires a change in diet. Since these changes take place slowly, they might not be recognizable. What is easily recognizable is weight gain. By continuing to feed your dog an adult-maintenance diet when he is slowing down metabolically, your dog will gain weight. Obesity in an older dog compounds the health problems that already accompany old age.

As your dog gets older, few of his organs function up to par. The kidneys slow down and the intestines become less efficient. These age-related factors are best handled with a change in diet and a change in feeding schedule to give smaller portions that are more easily digested. There is no single best diet for every older dog. While many dogs do well on light or senior diets, other dogs do better on puppy diets or special premium diets such as lamb and rice. Be sensitive to

your senior Bergamasco's diet, as this will help control other problems that may arise with your old friend.

### GRAIN-BASED DIETS

Some less expensive dog foods are based on grains and other plant proteins. While these products may appear to be attractively priced, many breeders prefer a diet based on animal proteins and believe that they are more conducive to your dog's health. Many grain-based diets rely on soy protein, which may cause flatulence (passing gas).

There are many cases, however, when your dog might require a special diet. These special requirements should only be recommended by your veterinarian.

## CHANGE IN DIET

As your dog's caretaker, you know the importance of keeping his diet consistent, but sometimes when you run out of food or if you're on vacation, you have to make a change quickly. Some dogs will experience digestive problems, but most will not. If you are planning on changing your dog's menu, do so gradually to ensure that your dog will not have any problems. Over a period of four to five days, slowly add some new food to your dog's old food, increasing the percentage of new food each day.

## WATER

Just as your dog needs proper nutrition from his food, water is an essential "nutrient" as well. Water keeps the dog's body properly hydrated and promotes normal function of the body's systems. During house-training, it is necessary to keep an eye on how much water your Bergamasco is drinking, but once he is reliably trained he should have access to clean fresh water at all times, especially if you feed dry food. Make certain that the dog's water bowl is clean, and change the water often.

## EXERCISE

The Bergamasco is quite an active dog, having been bred as a vigorous herding dog for centuries. The transition from working dog to sleeping pet is not easy for any natural, unspoiled breed. As such, the Bergamasco needs stimulation, mental and physical, in order to stay fit and sane. A sedentary lifestyle is as harmful to a dog as it is to a person, and a Bergamasco subjected to a "crated" lifestyle will not thrive. Owners certainly do not pick a breed like the Bergamasco solely for the allure of his remarkable coat! You have to want to spend time with this wholly engaging animal, and that means exercise. Exercising your Bergamasco can be enjoyable and healthy for both of you. Brisk walks, once the puppy reaches three or four months of age, will stimulate heart rates and build muscle for the growing dog. As the dog reaches adulthood, the speed and distance of the walks can be increased as long as they are both kept reasonable and comfortable for both of you.

# A Worthy Investment

**Veterinary studies have proven that a balanced high-quality diet pays off in your dog's coat quality, behavior and activity level. Invest in premium food for the maximum payoff with your dog.**

## DRINK, DRANK, DRUNK— MAKE IT A DOUBLE

In both humans and dogs, as well as other living organisms, water forms the major part of nearly every body tissue. Naturally, we take water for granted, but without it, life as we know it would cease.

For dogs, water is needed to keep their bodies functioning biochemically. Additionally, water is needed to replace the water lost while panting. Unlike humans, who are able to sweat to dissipate heat, dogs must pant to cool down, thereby losing the vital water that their bodies need to regulate their body temperatures. Humans lose electrolyte-containing products and other body-fluid components through sweating; dogs do not lose anything except water.

Water is essential always, but especially so when the weather is hot or humid or when your dog is exercising or working vigorously.

Play sessions and letting the dog run free in the fenced yard or other secure area under your supervision also are sufficient forms of exercise for the Bergamasco. Fetching games can be played indoors or out; these are excellent for giving your dog active play that he will enjoy. Chasing things that move comes naturally to dogs of all breeds. Some Bergamasco owners admit that their dogs prefer to "herd" balls rather than retrieve them, but this can be a great start! When your Bergamasco runs after the ball or object, praise him for picking it up and encourage him to bring it back to you for another throw. Never go to the object and pick it up yourself, or you'll soon find that you are the one retrieving the objects rather than the dog! If you choose to play games outdoors, you must have a securely fenced-in yard and/or have the dog attached to at least a 25-foot light line for security. You want your Bergamasco to run, but not run away!

Bear in mind that an overweight dog should never be suddenly over-exercised; instead, he should be encouraged to increase exercise slowly. Also, remember that not only is exercise essential to keep the dog's body fit, it is essential to his mental well-being. A bored dog will find something to do, which often manifests itself in some type of destructive

Play sessions are important to the physical and mental health of your dog. Don't overdo the exercise for a young puppy. Let him establish his own limits for physical activity.

behavior. In this sense, exercise is just as essential for the owner's mental well-being!

## GROOMING

When people first see a fully-coated mature Bergamasco, they immediately wonder how an owner can possibly take care of that coat. Most onlookers really believe that the owner has to sit with the dog for hours, weaving the hair to make it look the way it does.

Believe it or not, the Bergamasco's coat actually requires very little care, except for the occasional brushing and bathing. You can even brush the Bergamasco when the dog is mature and the hair has flocked together!

The Bergamasco's coat is forever changing, from the adorable, soft, fluffy puppy coat to the beginning flocking stage, which may start as early as 8 to 12 months of age. When this flocking (which I call the tangled, messy look) starts, it lasts until the dog is approximately two years old. At approximately three years old, the Bergamasco finally achieves the look that everyone has been waiting for!

The Bergamasco's coat is made up of hair, not fur, and is considered to be non-shedding. I would like to make it clear that the Bergamasco hair does not cord (cording is the twisting of hairs together to

Your local pet shop should have the grooming tools needed to keep your Bergamasco's coat in proper condition.

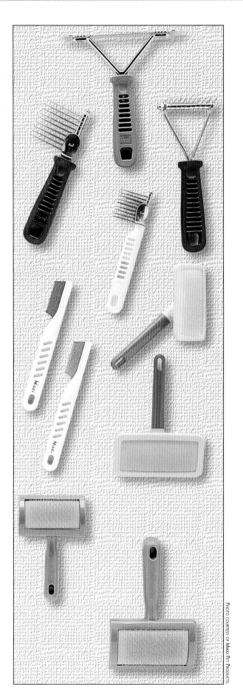

create a spiral strand as seen in the Hungarian Puli and Komondor). The Bergamasco's coat is very different in that the strands of hair weave together, creating flat layers of hair called "flocks." The definition of a flock is a tuft or lock of wool or hair. Each flock of hair ranges in width anywhere from 1.5 to 3 inches wide.

Before we can discuss each stage of coat development, you must first understand the formation of the Bergamasco's coat. The coat is made up of three types of hair: the undercoat, which is fine, dense and oily (not greasy) to the touch and forms a waterproof, protective layer; the goat hair, which looks like thin strands and is strong and harsh, likened to the coat of a goat; and the woolly top coat, which is finer and softer to the touch. The woolly hair and the goat hair weave together to create the flocks.

**DIFFERENT STAGES OF COAT CARE**
There is nothing more beautiful than watching the movement of the Bergamasco with all of the flocks flowing through the air. I have always said that the Bergamasco, unlike other breeds, is always changing, year after year, from the adorable, fluffy puppy stage, to the tangled youthful rebel stage, to the beautiful, majestic, mature Bergamasco. We have come to know and love all of the stages!

A Bergamasco's need for grooming changes as the coat develops. Although it is hard to imagine, the coat does not require as much grooming and care as you might expect.

### BIRTH TO TWO YEARS

Each dog develops at his own rate depending on his individual genetics. Whether you have a gray or black puppy, coat care is still

---

## GROOMING EQUIPMENT

Always purchase the best quality grooming equipment so that your tools will last for many years to come. Here are some basics:

- Pinbrush
- Slicker brush
- Scissors
- Rubber mat
- Dog shampoo
- Spray hose attachment
- Towels
- Blow dryer
- Ear cleaner
- Cotton balls
- Nail clippers

---

the same. It is acceptable to bathe your puppy once in a while or when the need arises; however, frequent bathing will dry out your puppy's skin and coat by removing the protective essential oils that keep the skin healthy and the coat clean. It is also important to keep your puppy free of any tangles or matting, especially in the beginning when the puppy coat is still present and the change to the beginning flocking stages has not occurred. A monthly brushing with a pinbrush will remove most tangles and debris.

At around eight to ten months, you will begin to notice the development of the longer smooth gray goat hair. This is the age at which the coat begins to get thicker, especially around the

A close-up of a mature Bergamasco coat. Note the different types of hair and how they weave together to create the "flocks."

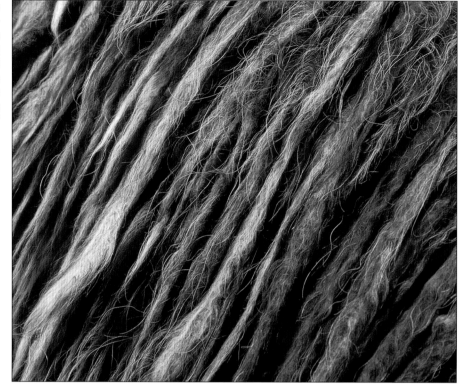

base of the tail. You will begin to notice thin smooth strands of hair along the back and base of the dog. This is what we call the goat hair. Now the beginning stages of flocking can occur. The goat hair together with the under-coat and the woolly coat come together to form shapeless clumps of immediate concern for the first-time Bergamasco owner. Most Bergamasco owners panic at this initial matting—flocking can be felt near the skin more than can be seen by the eye. Most owners find these first flocks

when brushing the coat and meeting resistance with the brush. From this point on, it is very important to put aside the brush and manually groom your Bergamasco by running your fingers through the dog's coat. Your dog should prefer your touch over any hand-held tool, and this is an excellent way to form a close bond with your Bergamasco.

Sometimes, in the early stages of the development of the flocks, there can be more woolly hair than usual, causing the

The Bergamasco coat starts to develop its characteristics after about eight months of age. This is a well-developed adult coat.

Brushing the young Bergamasco's coat keeps it free of tangles and debris. This should be done once a month during puppyhood, before the coat begins to mat.

softer, finer puppy hair to mat close to the skin. This type of mat should not occur at this stage. It is important to separate these areas by hand so that the skin is not pulled. When the flocks begin to take shape, you will notice that the base of the flock at the skin is never woven, but has straight non-woven strands of hair. This naturally creates a space between the dog's skin and the beginning formation of the flock. This is why the Bergamasco is not plagued with skin problems.

It also important to note at this stage that one must limit bathing to necessity only, as water on the coat causes the hair to become tighter to the skin, almost like a wool sweater shrinking. This makes it very difficult to separate the clumps into smaller groupings.

If the clumps of hair (new flocks) are larger than two to three fingers wide, or if there are different areas of hair binding together (creating matting and pulling the skin), you must simply tear the flocks with your fingers from the loose end (hair not attached to the skin) down to the skin. It is not important to worry about the shape or direction of the mats when tearing, but simply to avoid the coat from forming a solid mat over the body. It is important, however, at this stage not to make the flocks

too thin, for eventually the thin flocks can break and fall off. It is better to have wider flocks than thin ones. As the Bergamasco flocks get longer with age, the sheer weight of a thin flock will cause it to break off or be pulled off during typical dog play.

During the first year to almost the second, your Bergamasco looks unkempt and you may hear some comments like, "Why don't you groom that poor dog?" Once, when showing one of our young male dogs, the judge commented about the initial flocks feeling like ticks. Of course, we weren't selected as Best in Show that time!

Grooming a Bergamasco with a lot of woolly coat can be a quite an adventure, constantly splitting and re-splitting the coat to help set up the initial flocks. Many Bergamascos have coats that require minimal initial or ongoing care. Believe it or not, once you have set the initial flocks, they are taking shape every day as your dog matures. Remember that each flock will be different in width and texture, depending on how the ratio of the three different types of hair intertwine.

On a typical Bergamasco's body, you will notice that the distribution of the various types of hair is not consistent. On the base of the tail, the rear section of the trunk and the limbs, there is a vast amount of woolly hair.

You will generally notice woolly hair throughout the dog's coat, with the exception of the shoulders to the thorax, where there is only goat hair. The hair in this region has a smoother texture.

Generally speaking, when the Bergamasco is starting to flock, check throughout the body, down to the skin, by separating the hair with your hands to make a visual inspection. During the first year, large mats can develop behind and underneath the ears that will need to be torn into smaller flocks by hand. The limbs and chest need to watched carefully as well. We also check underneath at the front and back armpits to make sure there aren't any mats pulling the skin. The same method applies—tear too-large groupings into thinner flocks by hand.

### TWO TO THREE YEARS OF AGE

This is the period when the dog's flocks begin to separate. Although still short in length, the flocks will have a flat fan-like appearance in shape and be visibly noticeable on the topline. You must watch carefully for the flocks to become neither too thick or wide nor too thin. If the flocks become too wide, it is important to separate them into the chosen width using the previously discussed method of tearing from the loose end down to the skin. The splitting of the too-large flock should always be done with the hands; however, if need be, scissors will work as an extreme last resort.

### THREE YEARS OF AGE AND OVER

Once your dog is about three years of age, someone may come up to you and ask, "Is that a Komondor or a Hungarian Puli?" "Ah," you say to yourself, "finally my Bergamasco is becoming a Bergamasco!"

Once you have reached this period, you have reached the "promised land"—so enjoy and watch as the flocks continue to grow throughout the dog's life. As your dog matures, length and multiple layers of flocks will magically appear before your eyes. The Bergamasco coat at this stage should now consist of well-developed flocks, beginning from the topline and eventually settling on the sides of body. Do not pull at a flock that is a little too thin, as eventually it may attach itself to another one next to it. It is important, though, to keep a watch on the coat and split any flocks that become too wide.

One should be aware that generally the flocks are not the same size everywhere on the dog's body. Generally, the flocks on the saddle and base of the tail are thicker and wider due to the abundance of woolly coat. However, in areas around the

The mature coat of a champion Bergamasco is characterized by long flocks, not too wide, of different sizes, handsomely hanging down the body.

The "promised land" of the Bergamasco's coat development: multiple layers of flocks that begin at the dog's topline and hang down the sides of the body.

shoulder and neck, there is very little woolly hair; there is only goat hair, creating a smooth saddle. On the chest, the woolly coat is not as thick; therefore, the flocks should be thinner and not as wide as those on the trunk of the dog.

Remember that the amount of woolly coat and goat hair varies on different parts of the dog, creating different-sized flocks throughout the dog's body. On the dog's limbs, the flocks should all be uniform in size, hanging loose to the ground. On the head area around the eyes and muzzle, the hair is softer, hanging loosely over the eyes. The hair should always cover the eyes, creating a visor, which protects the eyes from the sun's rays. It usually takes up to five years for the Bergamasco coat to fully develop into layers upon layers of flocks that extend from the dog's shoulders to the paws.

### BATHING YOUR BERGAMASCO

The Bergamasco is generally a very clean dog; therefore, it is only necessary to bathe two or three times a year. The hair has natural oils that create a protective layer to help make the coat water- and dirt-resistant. Without oil for natural protection, the hair becomes dry and absorbs water as well as dirt more easily. The natural skin oil protects against dirt and dryness.

When the need arises, you can spot-bathe your dog in areas such as the whiskers and under the mouth, where food particles can accumulate. Other areas where dirt may collect are the paws, fronts of lower limbs, underneath the belly and behind the tail area, where you may find dry feces.

When washing your Bergamasco, it is important to use lots of water and gentle dog shampoo. There are now some excellent soap-free shampoos on the market today. The advantage to a detergent-based shampoo is that no residual detergent is left in the hair. When washing the coat, use plenty of warm water, wetting all the layers of the coat, especially the layers underneath. While rinsing, it is important not to leave any cleaning residue in the coat by constantly rinsing the flocks with water while squeezing or twisting the flocks to remove as much water as possible. The flocks, like a sponge, absorb a lot of water, and the more water you can squeeze, the faster the drying process will be.

It is always best to bathe your dog on a breezy warm day, so drying time can be kept to a minimum; otherwise, it can take two to three days to dry a fully-coated Bergamasco. If you use a hair dryer, never use a dryer designed for humans, as the heat is too hot for dog hair and can severely damage the coat. It is best to use a

**SOAP IT UP**

The use of human soap products like shampoo, bubble bath and hand soap can be damaging to a dog's coat and skin. Human products are too strong; they remove the protective oils coating the dog's hair and skin that make him water-resistant. Use only shampoo made especially for dogs. You may like to use a medicated shampoo, which will help to keep external parasites at bay.

commercial grooming dryer that offers different air flow attachments and has various temperature ranges.

### BRUSHING YOUR BERGAMASCO

Many people ask, "Can you brush that coat?" The answer is yes. An adult or puppy can be brushed. A puppy should have a monthly brushing to help remove small tangles and debris. A pinbrush should be used to brush the puppy coat. A pinbrush will not harm the coat or take out the undercoat. A slicker brush can be used on a fully-flocked and coated Bergamasco. The slicker brush will not damage the dense adult flocks but will remove the surface dirt that settles on the flocks. It is also very healthy to brush the adult coat occasionally; at this stage, the adult dogs seem to enjoy brushing and it helps to keep their coats nice and tidy.

Examine your pup's teeth regularly. They should appear strong, white and plaque-free. Report any retained puppy teeth to your vet.

The Bergamasco is a very simple, genuine dog, traits which are reflected in his coat. It is best to let the coat and dog develop as naturally and spontaneously as possible. Human intervention should be there to help the Bergamasco when necessary, but not there to change the overall appearance or characteristics that have been present and celebrated for centuries.

### EAR CLEANING

It is important to check the ears regularly and treat any ear problems accordingly. If you look into the Bergamasco's ear, it is usually pink in color. When you see a Bergamasco scratch his ear on a regular basis, you need to look into the ear. One of the signs of an ear infection is a dark brown discharge. You can usually treat a mild ear infection with a prepared boric and acetic acid solution. If the infection persists, your vet can prescribe an antibiotic ointment, which is usually effective.

Cleaning your dog's ears should be done regularly. Check for any foreign odors or ear mites when cleaning the ears.

### FOOT MAINTENANCE

The Bergamasco's feet should be checked for any possible stones or hard mud that can cause discomfort. Debris can lodge or mud can build up in the hair between the pads. If you notice that the dog is limping slightly or biting his feet, he may be indicating to you that there is some

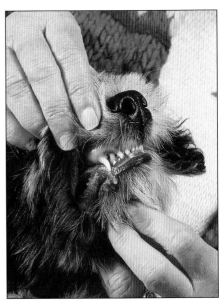

foreign object caught in his pad. For those who have snow in the winter, it is especially important to remove the ice chunks that can quickly settle under his paws, which can cause a cold burn if left in for long.

### TOOTH MAINTENANCE

By providing your dog with good chew toys from puppyhood through adulthood, you will help

A slicker brush removes the surface dirt from a fully-flocked Bergamasco. Most Bergamascos enjoy the stimulation that brushing provides.

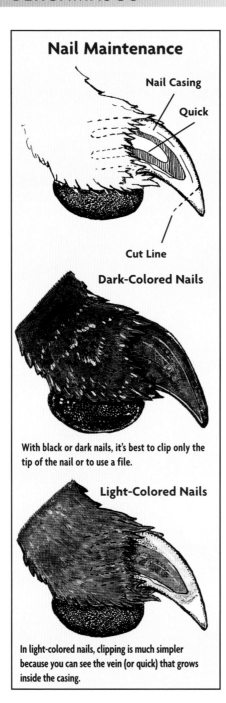

**Nail Maintenance**

Nail Casing

Quick

Cut Line

**Dark-Colored Nails**

With black or dark nails, it's best to clip only the tip of the nail or to use a file.

**Light-Colored Nails**

In light-colored nails, clipping is much simpler because you can see the vein (or quick) that grows inside the casing.

maintain his teeth and keep them healthy. There are various types of chew toys on the market, marrow bones available at your local butcher store and a variety of dense natural rubber chew toys available. These toys help keep your Bergamasco's teeth clean, remove plaque and massage his gums while he is happily playing.

Besides helping your dog with his daily chewing habits, you can occasionally brush his teeth by using a doggy toothbrush and a toothpaste formulated for dogs. The finger toothbrush, which is a soft pliable toothbrush that slips on your finger, is one of the easiest dog-friendly methods to use. If tartar or plaque does build up on the dog's teeth, a veterinary dentist may be necessary for dental care.

## TRAVELING WITH YOUR DOG

### CAR TRAVEL

You should accustom your Bergamasco to riding in a car at an early age. You may or may not take him in the car often, but at the very least he will need to go to the vet and you do not want these trips to be traumatic for the dog or troublesome for you. The safest way for a dog to ride in the car is in his crate. If he uses a crate in the house, you can use the same crate for travel.

Put the pup in the crate and see how he reacts. If he seems

uneasy, you can have a passenger hold him on his lap while you drive. Another option for car travel is a specially made safety harness for dogs, which straps the dog in much like a seat belt. Do not let the dog roam loose in the vehicle—this is very dangerous! If you should stop short, your dog can be thrown and injured. If the dog starts climbing on you and pestering you while you are driving, you will not be able to concentrate on the road. It is an unsafe situation for everyone— human and canine.

For long trips, bring along some water for the dog and be prepared to stop to let him relieve himself. Take with you whatever you need to clean up after him, including some paper towels and perhaps some old rags for use should he have a potty accident in the car or suffer from motion sickness.

### AIR TRAVEL
Contact your chosen airline before proceeding with travel plans that include your Bergamasco. The dog will be required to travel in a fiberglass crate and you should always check in advance with the airline regarding specific requirements for the crate, as well as any travel restrictions or heath certificates needed.

To help put the dog at ease, give him one of his favorite toys in the crate. Do not feed the dog

> **TRAVEL ALERT**
> Never leave your dog alone in the car. In hot weather, your dog can die from the high temperature inside a closed vehicle; even a car parked in the shade can heat up very quickly. Leaving the window open is dangerous as well since the dog can hurt himself trying to get out.

for several hours before the trip in order to minimize his need to relieve himself. Some airlines require you to provide documentation as to when the dog was last fed. In any case, a light meal is best. If your Bergamasco is going to be flying on a long flight, you may have to provide food and water and his bowls so that he can be attended to by the flight crew between legs of the journey.

Make sure your dog is properly identified and that your contact information appears on his ID tags and on his crate. Animals travel in a different area of the plane than human passengers, so every rule must be strictly followed so as to prevent the risk of getting separated from your dog.

### VACATIONS AND BOARDING
So you want to take a family vacation—and you want to include *all* members of the family. You would probably make arrangements for accommodations ahead of time anyway, but this is

Visit the boarding kennels in your area and pick a suitable facility well in advance of your travels.

especially important when traveling with a dog. You do not want to make an overnight stop at the only place around for miles, only to find out that they do not allow dogs. Also, you do not want to reserve a place for your family without confirming that you are traveling with a dog, because, if it is against their policy, you may end up without a place to stay.

Alternatively, if you are traveling and choose not to bring your Bergamasco, you will have to make arrangements for him while you are away. Some options are to take him to a friend's house to stay while you are gone, to have a trusted neighbor stop by often or stay at your house or to bring your dog to a reputable boarding kennel.

If you choose to board him at a kennel, you should visit in advance to see the facilities provided and where the dogs are kept. Are the dogs' areas spacious and kept clean? Talk to some of the employees and observe how they treat the dogs—do they spend time with the dogs, play with them, exercise them, etc.?

**ON-LEAD ONLY**
When traveling, never let your dog off-lead in a strange area. Your dog could run away out of fear, decide to chase a passing squirrel or cat or simply want to stretch his legs without restriction—if any of these happen, you might never see your canine friend again.

Also find out the kennel's policy on vaccinations and what they require. This is for all of the dogs' safety, since there is a greater risk of diseases being passed from dog to dog when dogs are kept together.

## IDENTIFICATION

Your Bergamasco is your valued companion and friend. That is why you always keep a close eye on him and you have made sure that he cannot escape from the yard or wriggle out of his collar and run away from you. However, accidents can happen and there may come a time when your dog unexpectedly becomes separated from you. If this unfortunate event should occur, the first thing on your mind will be finding him. Proper identification, including an ID tag and possibly a tattoo and/or a microchip, will increase the chances of his being returned to you safely and quickly.

## IDENTIFICATION OPTIONS

As puppies become more and more expensive, especially those puppies of high quality for showing and/or breeding, they have a greater chance of being stolen. The usual collar dog tag is, of course, easily removed. But there are two more permanent techniques that have become widely used for identification.

The puppy microchip implantation involves the injection of a small microchip, about the size of a corn kernel, under the skin of the dog. If your dog shows up at a clinic or shelter, or is offered for resale under less-than-savory circumstances, he can be positively identified by the microchip. The microchip is scanned, and a registry quickly identifies you as the owner.

Tattooing is done on various parts of the dog, from his belly to his ears. The number tattooed can be your telephone number, your dog's registration number or any other number that you can easily memorize. When professional dog thieves see a tattooed dog, they usually lose interest. For the safety of our dogs, no laboratory facility or dog broker will accept a tattooed dog as stock.

Discuss microchipping and tattooing with your veterinarian and breeder. Some vets perform these services on their own premises for a reasonable fee. To ensure that your dog's identification is effective, be certain that the dog is then properly registered with a legitimate national database.

Your dog should *never* be without an identifying dog tag on his everyday collar.

# TRAINING YOUR
# BERGAMASCO

Living with an untrained dog is a lot like owning a piano that you do not know how to play—it is a nice object to look at, but it does not do much more than that to bring you pleasure. Now try taking piano lessons, and suddenly the piano comes alive and brings forth magical sounds and rhythms that set your heart singing and your body swaying.

The same is true with your Bergamasco. Any dog is a big responsibility and, if not trained sensibly, may develop unacceptable behavior that annoys you or could even cause family friction.

To train your Bergamasco, you may like to enroll in an obedience class. Teach your dog good manners as you learn how and why he behaves the way he does. Find out how to communicate with your dog and how to recognize and understand his communications with you. Suddenly the dog takes on a new role in your life—he is clever, interesting, well behaved and fun to be with. He demonstrates his bond of devotion to you daily. In other words, your Bergamasco does wonders for your ego because he constantly reminds you that you are not only his leader, you are his hero!

Those involved with teaching dog obedience and counseling owners about their dogs' behavior have discovered some interesting facts about dog ownership. For

**REAP THE REWARDS**
If you start with a normal, healthy dog and give him time, patience and some carefully executed lessons, you will reap the rewards of that training for the life of the dog. And what a life it will be! The two of you will find immeasurable pleasure in the companionship you have built together with love, respect and understanding.

**THINK BEFORE YOU BARK**

Dogs are sensitive to their masters' moods and emotions. Use your voice wisely when communicating with your dog. Never raise your voice at your dog unless you are trying to correct him. "Barking" at your dog can become as meaningless as "dogspeak" is to you.

example, training dogs when they are puppies results in the highest rate of success in developing well-mannered and well-adjusted adult dogs. Training an older dog, from six months to six years of age, can produce almost equal results, providing that the owner accepts the dog's slower rate of learning capability and is willing to work patiently to help the dog succeed at developing to his fullest potential. Unfortunately, many owners of untrained adult dogs lack the patience factor, so they do not persist until their dogs are successful at learning particular behaviors.

Training a puppy aged 10 to 16 weeks (20 weeks at the most) is like working with a dry sponge in a pool of water. The pup soaks up whatever you show him and constantly looks for more things to do and learn. At this early age, his body is not yet producing hormones, and therein lies the reason for such a high rate of success. Without hormones, he is focused on his owners and not particularly interested in investigating other places, dogs, people, etc. You are his leader: his provider of food, water, shelter and security. He latches onto you and wants to stay close. He will usually follow you from room to room, will not let you out of his sight when you are outdoors with him and will respond in like manner to the people and animals you encounter. If you greet a friend warmly, he will be happy to

A trained puppy is a happy puppy... and a wonderful friend and companion.

**PAPER CAPER**

Never line your pup's sleeping area with newspaper. Puppy litters are usually raised on newspaper and, once in your home, the puppy will immediately associate newspaper with voiding. Never put newspaper on any floor while house-training, as this will only confuse the puppy. If you are paper-training him, use paper in his designated relief area only. Finally, restrict water intake after evening meals. Offer a few licks at a time—never let a Bergamasco of any age gulp water after meals.

greet the person as well. If, however, you are hesitant or anxious about the approach of a stranger, he will respond accordingly to you.

Once the puppy begins to produce hormones, his natural curiosity emerges and he begins to investigate the world around him. It is at this time when you may notice that the untrained dog begins to wander away from you and even ignore your commands

Breeders provide their pups with comfortable living quarters in which they can play, rest and snuggle up.

to stay close. When this behavior becomes a problem, you have two choices: get rid of the dog or train him. It is strongly urged that you choose the latter option.

You usually will be able to find obedience classes within a reasonable distance from your home, but you can also do a lot to train your dog yourself. Sometimes there are classes available, but the tuition is too costly. Whatever the circumstances, the solution to training your dog without formal obedience classes lies within the pages of this book.

This chapter is devoted to helping you train your Bergamasco at home. If the recommended procedures are followed faithfully, you may expect positive results that will prove rewarding both to you and your dog.

Whether your new charge is a puppy or a mature adult, the methods of teaching and the techniques we use in training basic behaviors are the same. After all, no dog, whether puppy or adult, likes harsh or inhumane methods. All creatures, however, respond favorably to gentle motivational methods and sincere praise and encouragement. Now let us get started.

**HOUSE-TRAINING**
You can train a puppy to relieve himself wherever you choose, but this must be somewhere suitable.

# CANINE DEVELOPMENT SCHEDULE

It is important to understand how and at what age a puppy develops into adulthood.
If you are a puppy owner, consult the following Canine Development Schedule to
determine the stage of development your puppy is currently experiencing.
This knowledge will help you as you work with the puppy in the weeks and months ahead.

| Period | Age | Characteristics |
|---|---|---|
| **First to Third** | **Birth to Seven Weeks** | Puppy needs food, sleep and warmth, and responds to simple and gentle touching. Needs mother for security and disciplining. Needs littermates for learning and interacting with other dogs. Pup learns to function within a pack and learns pack order of dominance. Begin socializing pup with adults and children for short periods. Pup begins to become aware of his environment. |
| **Fourth** | **Eight to Twelve Weeks** | Brain is fully developed. Pup needs socializing with outside world. Remove from mother and littermates. Needs to change from canine pack to human pack. Human dominance necessary. Fear period occurs between 8 and 12 weeks. Avoid fright and pain. |
| **Fifth** | **Thirteen to Sixteen Weeks** | Training and formal obedience should begin. Less association with other dogs, more with people, places, situations. Period will pass easily if you remember this is pup's change-to-adolescence time. Be firm and fair. Flight instinct prominent. Permissiveness and over-disciplining can do permanent damage. Praise for good behavior. |
| **Juvenile** | **Four to Eight Months** | Another fear period about 7 to 8 months of age. It passes quickly, but be cautious of fright and pain. Sexual maturity reached. Dominant traits established. Dog should understand sit, down, come and stay by now. |

NOTE: THESE ARE APPROXIMATE TIME FRAMES. ALLOW FOR INDIVIDUAL DIFFERENCES IN PUPPIES.

You should bear in mind from the outset that when your puppy is old enough to go out in public places, any canine deposits must be removed at once. You will always have to carry with you a small plastic bag or "poop-scoop."

Outdoor training includes such surfaces as grass, soil and cement. Indoor training usually means training your dog to newspaper. When deciding on the surface and location that you will

## MEALTIME

Mealtime should be a peaceful time for your puppy. Do not put his food and water bowls in a high-traffic area in the house. For example, give him his own little corner of the kitchen where he can eat undisturbed and where he will not be underfoot. Do not allow small children or other family members to disturb the pup when he is eating.

want your Bergamasco to use, be sure it is going to be permanent. Training your dog to grass and then changing your mind a few months later is extremely difficult for both dog and owner.

Next, choose the command you will use each and every time you want your puppy to void. "Hurry up" and "Let's go" are examples of commands commonly used by dog owners. Get in the habit of giving the puppy your chosen relief command before you take him out. That way, when he becomes an adult, you will be able to determine if he wants to go out when you ask him. A confirmation will be signs of interest, such as wagging his tail, watching you intently, going to the door, etc.

### PUPPY'S NEEDS

Your puppy needs to relieve himself after play periods, after each meal, after he has been sleeping and at any time he indicates that he is looking for a place to urinate or defecate. The urinary and intestinal tract muscles of very young puppies are not fully developed. Therefore, like human babies, puppies need to relieve themselves frequently.

Take your puppy out often—every hour for the first week or so after he comes home and always immediately after sleeping and eating. The older the puppy, the less often he will need to relieve himself. Finally, as a mature healthy adult, he will require only three to five relief trips per day.

## HOUSING

Since the types of housing and control you provide for your puppy have a direct relationship on the success of house-training, we consider the various aspects of both before we begin training.

Taking a new puppy home and turning him loose in your house can be compared to turning a child loose in a sports arena and telling the child that the place is all his! The sheer enormity of the place would be too much for him to handle. Instead, offer the puppy clearly defined areas where he can play, sleep, eat and live. A room of the house where the family gathers is the most obvious choice. Puppies are social animals and need to feel a part of the pack right from the start. Hearing your voice, watching you while you are doing things and smelling you nearby are all positive reinforcers that he is now a member of your pack. Usually a family room, the kitchen or a nearby adjoining breakfast area is ideal for providing safety and security for both puppy and owner.

Within the designated room, there should be a smaller area that the puppy can call his own. An alcove, a wire or fiberglass dog crate or a gated corner from which he can view the activities of his

> **TAKE THE LEAD**
> Do not carry your dog to his relief area. Lead him there on a leash or, better yet, encourage him to follow you to the spot. If you start carrying him to his spot, you might end up doing this routine forever and your dog will have the satisfaction of having trained *you*.

new family will be fine. The size of the area or crate is the key factor here. The area must be large enough so that the puppy can lie down and stretch out, as well as stand up, without rubbing his head on the top. At the same time, it must be small enough so that he cannot relieve himself at one end and sleep at the other without coming into contact with his droppings. Dogs are, by nature, clean animals and will not remain close to their relief areas unless forced to do so. In those cases, they then become dirty dogs and usually remain that way for life.

The dog's designated area should contain clean bedding and a toy. Water must always be available, in a non-spill container, although you should keep an eye on your pup's water intake during house-training so you can predict when he will need to go out.

## CONTROL

By *control*, we mean helping the puppy to create a lifestyle pattern that will be compatible to that of his human pack (you!). Just as we guide little children to learn our way of life, we must show the puppy when it is time to play, eat, sleep, exercise and even entertain himself.

Your puppy should always sleep in his crate. He should also learn that, during times of household confusion and excessive human activity, such as at breakfast when family members are preparing for the day, he can play by himself in relative safety and comfort in his designated area.

# THE SUCCESS METHOD

Success that comes by luck is usually short-lived. Success that comes by well-thought-out proven methods is often more easily achieved and permanent. This is the Success Method. It is designed to give you, the puppy owner, a simple yet proven way to help your puppy develop clean living habits and a feeling of security in his new environment.

## 6 Steps to Successful Crate Training

**1** Tell the puppy "Crate time!" and place him in the crate with a small treat (a piece of cheese or half of a biscuit). Let him stay in the crate for five minutes while you are in the same room. Then release him and praise lavishly. Never release him when he is fussing. Wait until he is quiet before you let him out.

**2** Repeat Step 1 several times a day.

**3** The next day, place the puppy in the crate as before. Let him stay there for ten minutes. Do this several times.

**4** Continue building time in five-minute increments until the puppy stays in his crate for 30 minutes with you in the room. Always take him to his relief area after prolonged periods in his crate.

**5** Now go back to Step 1 and let the puppy stay in his crate for five minutes, this time while you are out of the room.

**6** Once again, build crate time in five-minute increments with you out of the room. When the puppy will stay willingly in his crate (he may even fall asleep!) for 30 minutes with you out of the room, he will be ready to stay in it for several hours at a time.

Each time you leave the puppy alone, he should understand exactly where he is to stay.

Puppies are chewers. They cannot tell the difference between things like lamp cords, television wires, shoes, table legs, etc. Chewing into a television wire, for example, can be fatal to the puppy, while a shorted wire can start a fire in the house. If the puppy chews on the arm of the chair when he is left alone, you will probably discipline him angrily when you get home. Thus, he makes the association that your coming home means he is going to be punished. (He will not remember chewing the chair and is incapable of making the association of the discipline with his naughty deed.) Accustoming the pup to his designated area not only keeps him safe but also avoids his engaging in destructive behaviors when you are not around.

Times of excitement, such as special occasions, family parties,

etc., can be fun for the puppy, providing that he can view the activities from the security of his designated area. He is not underfoot and he is not being fed all sorts of tidbits that will probably cause him stomach distress, yet he still feels a part of the fun.

*Puppies will need to relieve themselves after* every *nap. Supervise your puppy indoors so that you always know his needs.*

### SCHEDULE

Your puppy should be taken to his relief area each time he is released from his designated area, after meals, after play sessions and when he first awakens in the morning (at age 12 weeks, this can mean 5 a.m.!). The puppy will indicate that he's ready "to go" by circling or sniffing busily—do not misinterpret these signs. When you first bring your puppy home, a routine of taking him out every hour is necessary. As the puppy grows, he will be able to wait for longer periods of time.

Keep trips to his relief area short. Stay no more than five or six minutes and then return to the house. If he goes during that time,

### HONOR AND OBEY

Dogs are the most honorable animals in existence. They consider another species (humans) as their own. They interface with you. You are their leader. Puppies perceive children to be on their level; their actions around small children are different from their behavior around their adult masters.

praise him lavishly and take him indoors immediately. If he does not, but he has an accident when you go back indoors, pick him up immediately, say "No! No!" and return to his relief area. Wait a few minutes, then return to the house again. Never hit a puppy or rub his face in urine or excrement when he has had an accident!

Once indoors, put the puppy in his crate until you have had time to clean up his accident. Then, release him to the family

area and watch him more closely than before. Chances are, his accident was a result of your not picking up his signal or waiting too long before offering him the opportunity to relieve himself. Never hold a grudge against the puppy for accidents.

Let the puppy learn that going outdoors means it is time to relieve himself, not to play. Once trained, he will be able to play indoors and out and still differentiate between the times for play versus the times for relief.

Help him develop regular hours for naps, being alone, playing by himself and just resting, all in his crate. Encourage him to entertain himself while you are busy with your activities. Let him learn that having you near is comforting, but it is not your main purpose in life to provide him with undivided attention.

Each time you put your puppy in his own area, use the same command, whatever suits best. Soon he will run to his crate or special area when he hears you say those words.

Crate training provides safety for you, the puppy and the home. It also provides the puppy with a feeling of security, and that helps the puppy achieve self-confidence and clean habits. Remember that one of the primary ingredients in house-training your puppy is control. Regardless of your lifestyle, there will always be

### HOW MANY TIMES A DAY?

| AGE | RELIEF TRIPS |
| --- | --- |
| To 14 weeks | 10 |
| 14–22 weeks | 8 |
| 22–32 weeks | 6 |
| Adulthood | 4 |
| (dog stops growing) | |

These are estimates, of course, but they are a guide to the *minimum* number of opportunities a dog should have each day to relieve himself.

occasions when you will need to have a place where your dog can stay and be happy and safe. Crate training is the answer for now and in the future.

In conclusion, a few key elements are really all you need for a successful house-training method—consistency, frequency, praise, control and supervision. By following these procedures with a normal, healthy puppy, you and the puppy will soon be past the stage of "accidents" and ready to move on to a clean and rewarding life together.

## ROLES OF DISCIPLINE, REWARD AND PUNISHMENT

Discipline, training one to act in accordance with rules, brings order to life. It is as simple as that. Without discipline, particularly in a group society, chaos will reign supreme and the group will eventually perish. Humans and canines are social animals and need some form of discipline in order to function effectively. They must procure food, reproduce to keep their species going and protect their home base and their young. If there were no discipline in the lives of social animals, they would eventually die from starvation and/or predation by other stronger animals.

In the case of domestic canines, discipline in their lives is needed in order for them to understand how their pack (you

**CALM DOWN**

Dogs will do anything for your attention. If you reward the dog when he is calm and attentive, you will develop a well-mannered dog. If, on the other hand, you greet your dog excitedly and encourage him to wrestle with you, the dog will greet you the same way and you will have a hyperactive dog on your hands.

and other family members) functions and how they must act in order to survive.

A large humane society in a highly populated area recently surveyed dog owners regarding their satisfaction with their relationships with their dogs. People who had trained their dogs were 75% more satisfied with their pets than those who had never trained their dogs.

**PLAN TO PLAY**

The puppy should also have regular play and exercise sessions when he is with you or a family member. Exercise for a very young puppy can consist of a short walk around the house or yard. Playing can include fetching games with a large ball or a special toy. (All puppies teethe and need soft things upon which to chew.) Remember to restrict play periods to indoors within his living area (the family room, for example) until he is completely house-trained.

Dr. Edward Thorndike, a noted psychologist, established *Thorndike's Theory of Learning*, which states that a behavior that results in a pleasant event tends

Mundane lessons make for a bored Bergamasco. Keep the dog's attention with short, enjoyable training sessions and plenty of time to play!

to be repeated. Conversely, a behavior that results in an unpleasant event tends not to be repeated. It is this theory upon which most training methods are based today. For example, if you manipulate a dog to perform a specific behavior and reward him for doing it, he is likely to do it again because he enjoyed the end result.

Occasionally, punishment, a penalty inflicted for an offense, is necessary. The best type of punishment often comes from an outside source. For example, a child is told not to touch the oven because he may get burned. He disobeys and touches the oven. In doing so, he receives a burn. From that time on, he respects the heat of the oven and avoids contact with it. Therefore, a behavior that results in an unpleasant event tends not to be repeated.

A good example of a dog learning the hard way is the dog who chases the house cat. He is told many times to leave the cat alone, yet he persists in teasing the cat. Then, one day, the dog begins chasing the cat but the cat turns and swipes a claw across the dog's face, leaving the dog with a painful gash on his nose. The final result is that the dog stops chasing the cat. This is another example of how a behavior that results in an unpleasant event tends not to be repeated.

## TRAINING EQUIPMENT

### COLLAR AND LEAD
For a Bergamasco, the collar and lead that you use for training must be ones with which you are easily able to work, not too heavy for the dog and perfectly safe.

### TREATS
Have a bag of treats on hand; something nutritious and easy to swallow works best. Use a soft treat, a chunk of cheese or a piece of cooked chicken rather than a dry biscuit. By the time the dog has finished chewing a dry treat, he will forget why he is being rewarded in the first place!

Using food rewards, it should be noted, will not teach a dog to beg at the table—the only way to teach a dog to beg at the table is to give him food from the table. In training, rewarding the dog with a food treat will help him associate praise and the treats with learning new behaviors that obviously please his owner.

## TRAINING BEGINS: ASK THE DOG A QUESTION
In order to teach your dog anything, you must first get his attention. After all, he cannot learn anything if he is looking away from you with his mind on something else.

To get your dog's attention, ask him "School?" and immediately walk over to him and give

## PARENTAL GUIDANCE
Training a dog is a life experience. Many parents admit that much of what they know about raising children they learned from caring for their dogs. Dogs respond to love, fairness and guidance, just as children do. Become a good dog owner and you may become an even better parent.

him a treat as you tell him "Good dog." Wait a minute or two and repeat the routine, this time with a treat in your hand as you approach within a foot of the dog. Do not go directly to him, but stop about a foot short of him and hold out the treat as you ask "School?" He will see you approaching with a treat in your hand and most likely begin walking toward you. As you meet, give him the treat and praise again.

The third time, ask the question, have a treat in your hand and walk only a short distance toward the dog so that he must walk almost all the way to you. As he reaches you, give him the treat and praise again.

By this time, the dog will probably be getting the idea that if he pays attention to you, especially when you ask that question, it will pay off in treats and enjoyable activities for him. In other words, he learns that "school" means doing great things with you that are fun and that result in positive attention for him.

Remember that the dog does not understand your verbal language; he only recognizes sounds. Your question translates to a series of sounds for him, and those sounds become the signal to go to you and pay attention. The dog learns that if he does this, he will get to interact with you plus receive treats and praise.

## THE BASIC COMMANDS

### TEACHING SIT

Now that you have the dog's attention, attach his lead and hold it in your left hand, and hold a food treat in your right hand. Place your food hand at the dog's nose and let him lick the treat but not take it from you. Say "Sit" and slowly raise your food hand from in front of the dog's nose up over his head so that he is looking at the ceiling. As he bends his head upward, he will have to bend his knees to maintain his balance. As he bends his knees, he will assume a sit position. At that point, release the food treat and praise lavishly with comments such as "Good dog! Good sit!" Remember to always praise enthusiastically, because dogs relish verbal praise from their owners and feel so proud of themselves whenever they accomplish a behavior.

Incidentally, you will not use food forever in getting the dog to obey your commands. Food is only used to teach new behaviors and, once the dog knows what

---

### LANGUAGE BARRIER

Dogs do not understand our language and have to rely on tone of voice more than just words or sound. They can be trained to react to a certain sound, at a certain volume. If you say "No, Oliver" in a very soft, pleasant voice, it will not have the same meaning as "No, Oliver!!" when you raise your voice.

You should never use the dog's name during a reprimand, just the command "No! " You never want the dog to associate his name with a negative experience or reprimand.

you want when you give a specific command, you will wean him off the food treats but still maintain the verbal praise. After all, you will always have your voice with you, and there will be many times when you have no food rewards but expect the dog to obey.

## TEACHING DOWN

Teaching the down exercise is easy when you understand how the dog perceives the down position, and it is very difficult when you do not. Dogs perceive the down position as a submissive one; therefore, teaching the down exercise by using a forceful method can sometimes make the dog develop such a fear of the down that he either runs away when you say "Down" or he attempts to snap at the person who tries to guide him down.

Have the dog sit close alongside your left leg, facing in the same direction as you are. Hold the lead in your left hand and a food treat in your right. Now place your left hand lightly on the top of the dog's shoulders where they meet above the spinal cord. Do not push down on the dog's shoulders; simply rest your left hand there so you can guide the dog to lie down close to your left leg rather than to swing away from your side when he drops.

Now place the food hand at the dog's nose, say "Down" very

**DOUBLE JEOPARDY**
A dog in jeopardy never lies down. He stays alert on his feet because instinct tells him that he may have to run away or fight for his survival. Therefore, if a dog feels threatened or anxious, he will not lie down. Consequently, it is important to keep the dog calm and relaxed as he learns the down exercise.

softly (almost a whisper) and slowly lower the food hand to the dog's front feet. When the food hand reaches the floor, begin moving it forward along the floor in front of the dog. Keep talking softly to the dog, saying things like, "Do you want this treat? You can do this, good dog." Your reassuring tone of voice will help calm the dog as he tries to follow the food hand in order to get the treat.

When the dog's elbows touch the floor, release the food and praise softly. Try to get the dog to maintain that down position for several seconds before you let him sit up again. The goal here is to get the dog to settle down and not feel threatened in the down position.

### TEACHING STAY

It is easy to teach the dog to stay in either a sit or a down position. Again, we use food and praise during the teaching process as we help the dog to understand exactly what it is that we are expecting him to do.

To teach the sit/stay, start with the dog sitting on your left side as before and hold the lead in your left hand. Have a food treat in your right hand and place your food hand at the dog's nose. Say "Stay" and step out on your right foot to stand directly in front of the dog, toe to toe, as he licks and nibbles the treat. Be sure to keep his head facing upward to maintain the sit position. Count to five and then swing around to stand next to the dog again with him on your left. As soon as you get back to the original position, release the food and praise lavishly.

"Where are you?" will become your pup's favorite question, promising an exciting and rewarding game with his family.

To teach the down/stay, do the down as previously described. As soon as the dog lies down, say "Stay" and step out on your right foot just as you did in the sit/stay. Count to five and then return to stand beside the dog with him on your left side. Release the treat and praise as always.

Within a week or ten days, you can begin to add a bit of distance between you and your dog when you leave him. When you do, use your left hand open with the palm facing the dog as a stay signal, much the same as the hand signal a police officer uses to stop traffic at an intersection. Hold the food treat in your right hand as before, but this time the food will not be touching the dog's nose. He will watch the food hand and quickly learn that he is going to get that treat as soon as you return to his side.

When you can stand 3 feet away from your dog for 30 seconds, you can then begin building time and distance in both stays. Eventually, the dog can be expected to remain in the stay position for prolonged periods of time until you return to him or call him to you. Always praise lavishly when he stays.

TEACHING COME

If you make teaching "come" an exciting experience, you should never have a "student" that does not love the game or that fails to

> **KEEP SMILING**
> Never train your dog, puppy or adult, when you are angry or in a sour mood. Dogs are very sensitive to human feelings, especially anger, and if your dog senses that you are angry or upset, he will connect your anger with his training and learn to resent or fear his training sessions.

come when called. The secret, it seems, is never to teach the word "come."

At times when an owner most wants his dog to come when called, the owner is likely to be upset or anxious and he allows these feelings to come through in the tone of his voice when he calls his dog. Hearing that desperation in his owner's voice, the dog fears the results of going to him and therefore either disobeys outright or runs in the opposite direction. The secret, therefore, is to teach the dog a game and, when you want him to come to you, simply play the game. It is practically a no-fail solution!

To begin, have several members of your family take a few food treats and each go into a different room in the house. Everyone takes turns calling the dog, and each person should celebrate the dog's finding him with a treat and lots of happy praise. When a person calls the dog, he is actually inviting the dog to find

### "COME" . . . BACK

Never call your dog to come to you for a correction or scold him when he reaches you. That is the quickest way to turn a come command into "Go away fast!" Dogs think only in the present tense, and your dog will connect the scolding with coming to you, not with the misbehavior of a few moments earlier.

him and to get a treat as a reward for "winning."

A few turns of the "Where are you?" game and the dog will understand that everyone is playing the game and that each person has a big celebration awaiting the dog's success at locating him or her. Once the dog

learns to love the game, simply calling out "Where are you?" will bring him running from wherever he is when he hears that all-important question.

The come command is recognized as one of the most important things to teach a dog, but there are trainers who work with thousands of dogs and never teach the actual word "come." Yet these dogs will race to respond to a person who uses the dog's name followed by "Where are you?" For example, a woman has a 12-year-old companion dog who went blind, but who never fails to locate her owner when asked, "Where are you?"

Children, in particular, love to play this game with their dogs. Children can hide in smaller places like a shower stall or bathtub, behind a bed or under a table. The dog needs to work a little bit harder to find these hiding places, but, when he does, he loves to celebrate with a treat and a tussle with a favorite youngster.

### TEACHING HEEL

Heeling means that the dog walks beside the owner without pulling. It takes time and patience on the owner's part to succeed at teaching the dog that he (the owner) will not proceed unless the dog is walking calmly beside him. Neither pulling out ahead on the lead nor lagging behind is acceptable.

Begin by holding the lead in your left hand as the dog sits beside your left leg. Move the loop end of the lead to your right hand, but keep your left hand short on the lead so that it keeps the dog in close next to you.

Say "Heel" and step forward on your left foot. Keep the dog close to you and take three steps. Stop and have the dog sit next to you in what we now call the heel position. Praise verbally, but do not touch the dog. Hesitate a moment and begin again with "Heel," taking three steps and stopping, at which point the dog is told to sit again.

### PRACTICE MAKES PERFECT!

- Have training lessons with your dog every day in several short segments—three to five times a day for a few minutes at a time is ideal.
- Do not have long practice sessions. The dog will become easily bored.
- Never practice when you are tired, ill, worried or in an otherwise negative mood. This will transmit to the dog and may have an adverse effect on his performance.

Think fun, short and above all *positive!* End each session on a high note, rather than a failed exercise, and make sure to give a lot of praise. Enjoy the training and help your dog enjoy it, too.

Your goal here is to have the dog walk those three steps without pulling on the lead. Once he will walk calmly beside you for three steps without pulling, increase the number of steps you take to five. When he will walk politely beside you while you take five steps, you can increase the length of your walk to ten steps. Keep increasing the length of your stroll until the dog will walk quietly beside you without pulling as long as you want him to heel. When you stop heeling, indicate to the dog that the exercise is over by verbally praising as you pet him and say "OK, good dog." The "OK" is used as a release word, meaning that the exercise is finished and the dog is free to relax.

If you are dealing with a dog who insists on pulling you around, simply "put on your brakes" and stand your ground until the dog realizes that the two of you are not going anywhere until he is beside you and moving at your pace, not his. It may take some time just standing there to convince the dog that you are the leader and that you will be the one to decide on the direction and speed of your travel.

Each time the dog looks up at you or slows down to give a slack lead between the two of you, quietly praise him and say, "Good heel. Good dog." Eventu-

**HEELING WELL**
Teach your dog to heel in an enclosed area. Once you think the dog will obey reliably and you want to attempt advanced obedience exercises such as off-lead heeling, test him in a fenced-in area so he cannot run away.

ally, the dog will begin to respond and within a few days he will be walking politely beside you without pulling on the lead. At first, the training sessions should be kept short and very positive; soon the dog will be able to walk nicely with you for increasingly longer distances. Remember also to give the dog free time and the opportunity to run and play when you have finished heel practice.

**WEANING OFF FOOD IN TRAINING**
Food is used in training new behaviors. Once the dog understands what behavior goes with a specific command, it is time to start weaning him off the food treats. At first, give a treat after each exercise. Then, start to give a treat only after every other exercise. Vary the times when you offer a food reward and the times when you only offer praise so that the dog will never know when he is going to receive both food and praise and when he is going to receive only praise. This is called

a variable-ratio reward system. It proves successful because there is always the chance that the owner will produce a treat, so the dog never stops trying for that reward. No matter what, *always* give verbal praise.

**OBEDIENCE CLASSES**
It is a good idea to enroll in an obedience class if one is available in your area. If yours is a show dog, conformation training classes would be more appropriate. Many areas have dog clubs that offer basic obedience training as well as preparatory classes for obedience competition. There are also local dog trainers who offer similar classes.

At obedience trials, dogs can earn titles at various levels of competition. The beginning levels of obedience competition include basic behaviors such as sit, down, heel, etc. The more advanced levels of competition include jumping, retrieving, scent discrimination and signal work. The advanced levels require a dog and owner to put a lot of time and effort into their training. The titles that can be earned at these levels of competition are very prestigious.

**OTHER ACTIVITIES FOR LIFE**
Whether a dog is trained in the structured environment of a class or alone with his owner at home, there are many activities that can

bring fun and rewards to both owner and dog once they have mastered basic control.

Teaching the dog to help out around the home, in the yard or on the farm provides great satisfaction to both dog and owner. In addition, the dog's help makes life a little easier for his owner and raises his stature as a valued companion to his family. It helps give the dog a purpose by occupying his mind and providing an outlet for his energy.

If you are interested in participating in organized competition with your Bergamasco, there are activities other than obedience in which you and your dog can become involved. Bergamasco owners can consider such endeavors as agility trials, herding events and obedience trials. Agility, likely the most popular of these, is a sport in which dogs run through an obstacle course that includes various jumps, tunnels and other exercises to test the dog's speed and coordination. The owners run beside their dogs to give commands and to guide them through the course. Although competitive, the focus is on fun—it's fun to do, fun to watch and great exercise. Since the Bergamasco derives from herding dogs and still retains his herding instincts, owners should investigate herding trials as well by contacting a nearby breed or herding-dog club.

## COMMAND STANCE
Stand up straight and authoritatively when giving your dog commands. Do not issue commands when lying on the floor or lying on your back on the sofa. If you are on your hands and knees when you give a command, your dog will think you are positioning yourself to play.

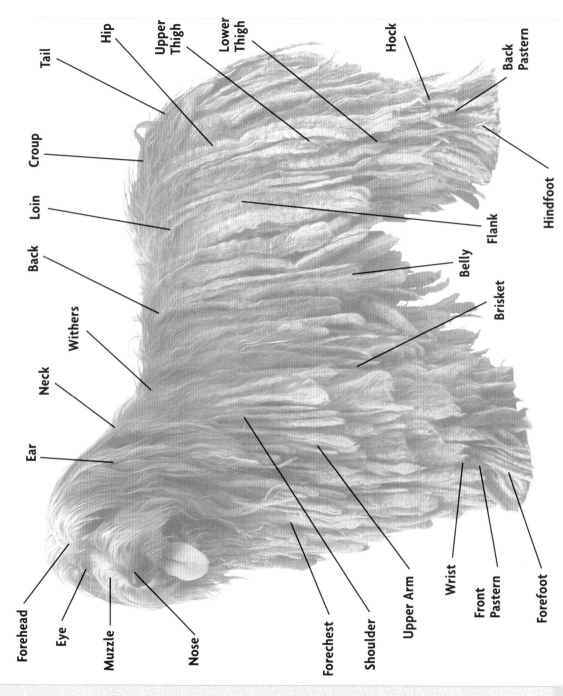

Tail

Hip

Upper Thigh

Lower Thigh

Hock

Back Pastern

Croup

Loin

Flank

Hindfoot

Back

Belly

Withers

Brisket

Neck

Ear

Forehead

Eye

Muzzle

Nose

Forechest

Shoulder

Upper Arm

Wrist

Front Pastern

Forefoot

# PHYSICAL STRUCTURE OF THE BERGAMASCO

Dogs can suffer from many of the same physical illnesses as people. They might even share many of the same psychological problems. Since people usually know more about human diseases than canine maladies, many of the terms used in this chapter will be familiar but not necessarily those used by veterinarians. We will use the term *x-ray*, instead of the more acceptable term *radiograph*. We will also use the familiar term *symptoms* even though dogs don't have symptoms, which are verbal descriptions of the patient's feelings; dogs have *clinical signs*. Since dogs can't speak, we have to look for clinical signs...but we still use the term *symptoms* in this book.

As a general rule, medicine is *practiced*. That term is not arbitrary. Medicine is a constantly changing art as we learn more and more about genetics, electronic aids (like CAT scans and MRIs) and daily laboratory advances. There are many dog maladies, like canine hip dysplasia, which are not universally treated in the same manner. For example, some veterinarians opt for surgery more often than others do.

## SELECTING A QUALIFIED VET

Your selection of a veterinarian should be based not only upon personality and excellence in his field but also upon his convenience to your home. You want a vet who is close because you might have emergencies or need to make multiple visits for treatments. You want a vet who has services that you might require such as tattooing and boarding, who makes the latest pet supplies available and of course who has a good reputation for ability and responsiveness. There is nothing more frustrating than having to wait to get a response from your veterinarian.

All vets are licensed and their diplomas and/or certificates should be displayed in their waiting rooms. Your vet will deal with all aspects of your dog's routine health care and maintenance, including check-ups, illnesses and injuries, the promotion of health (for example, by vaccination) and routine surgeries. There are, however, many veterinary specialties that require further studies and internships. These include specialists in heart problems (veterinary cardiologists), skin problems (veterinary

1. Esophagus
2. Lungs
3. Gall Bladder
4. Liver
5. Kidney
6. Stomach
7. Intestines
8. Urinary Bladder

# INTERNAL ORGANS OF THE BERGAMASCO

dermatologists), tooth and gum problems (veterinary dentists), eye problems (veterinary ophthalmologists) and x-rays (veterinary radiologists), as well as vets who have specialties in bones, muscles or certain organs. When the problem affecting your dog is serious, it is not unusual or impudent to get another medical opinion, although it is courteous to advise the vets concerned about this. You might also want to compare costs among several vets. Sophisticated health care and veterinary

**Breakdown of Veterinary Income by Category**

| 2% | Dentistry |
| 4% | Radiology |
| 12% | Surgery |
| 15% | Vaccinations |
| 19% | Laboratory |
| 23% | Examinations |
| 25% | Medicines |

A typical vet's income, categorized according to services performed. This survey dealt with small-animal (pets) practices.

## PET ADVANTAGES
If you do not intend to show or breed your new puppy, your veterinarian will probably recommend that you spay your female or neuter your male. Some people believe neutering leads to weight gain, but if you feed and exercise your dog properly, this is easily avoided. Spaying or neutering can actually have many positive outcomes, such as:
• training becomes easier, as the dog focuses less on the urge to mate and more on you!
• females are protected from unplanned pregnancy as well as ovarian and uterine cancers.
• males are guarded from testicular tumors and have a reduced risk of developing prostate cancer.
   Talk to your vet regarding the right age to spay/neuter and other aspects of the procedure.

services can be very costly. It is not infrequent that important decisions are based upon financial considerations.

### PREVENTATIVE MEDICINE
It is much easier, less costly and more effective to practice preventative medicine than to fight bouts of illness and disease. Properly bred puppies come from parents who were selected based upon their genetic-disease profiles. Their dam should have been vaccinated, free of all internal and external parasites and properly nourished. The dam can pass on disease resistance to her puppies, which can last for eight to ten weeks, but she can also pass on parasites and many infections. For these reasons, it is advisable to learn as much about the dam as you possibly can.

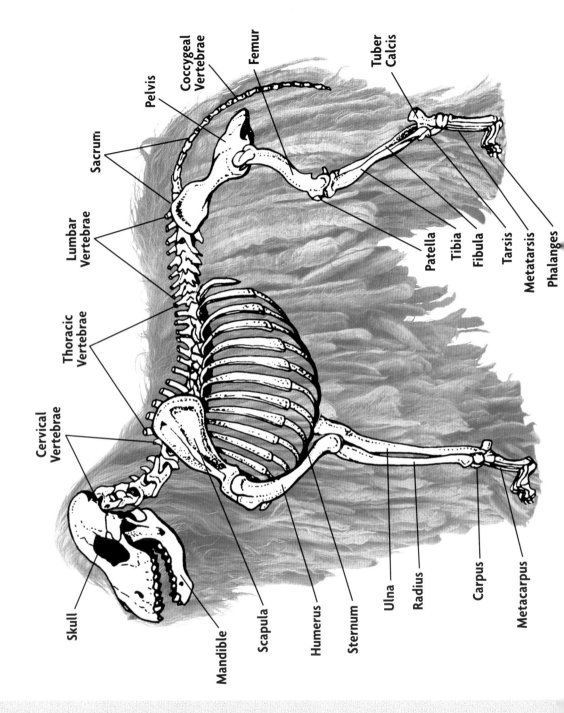

Coccygeal Vertebrae

Femur

Tuber Calcis

Pelvis

Sacrum

Patella

Tibia

Fibula

Tarsis

Metatarsis

Phalanges

Lumbar Vertebrae

Thoracic Vertebrae

Cervical Vertebrae

Skull

Mandible

Scapula

Humerus

Sternum

Ulna

Radius

Carpus

Metacarpus

# SKELETAL STRUCTURE OF THE BERGAMASCO

**THE SAME ALLERGIES**
Chances are that you and your dog will have the same allergies. Your allergies are readily recognizable and usually easily treated. Your dog's allergies may be masked.

**WEANING TO BRINGING PUPPY HOME**
Puppies should be weaned by the time they are about two months old. A Bergamasco puppy that remains for at least 12 weeks with his dam and littermates usually adapts better to other dogs and

people later in life. Some new owners have their puppies examined by veterinarians immediately, which is a good idea. Vaccination programs usually begin when the puppy is very young.

The puppy will have his teeth examined, and have his skeletal conformation and general health checked prior to certification by the veterinarian. Puppies in certain breeds may have problems with their kneecaps, cataracts and other eye problems, heart murmurs or undescended testicles. Your vet might also have training in

# DISEASE REFERENCE CHART

| | What is it? | What causes it? | Symptoms |
|---|---|---|---|
| **Leptospirosis** | Severe disease that affects the internal organs; can be spread to people. | A bacterium, which is often carried by rodents, that enters through mucous membranes and spreads quickly throughout the body. | Range from fever, vomiting and loss of appetite in less severe cases to shock, irreversible kidney damage and possibly death in most severe cases. |
| **Rabies** | Potentially deadly virus that infects warm-blooded mammals. | Bite from a carrier of the virus, mainly wild animals. | 1st stage: dog exhibits change in behavior, fear. 2nd stage: dog's behavior becomes more aggressive. 3rd stage: loss of coordination, trouble with bodily functions. |
| **Parvovirus** | Highly contagious virus, potentially deadly. | Ingestion of the virus, which is usually spread through the feces of infected dogs. | Most common: severe diarrhea. Also vomiting, fatigue, lack of appetite. |
| **Canine cough** | Contagious respiratory infection. | Combination of types of bacteria and virus. Most common: *Bordetella bronchiseptica* bacteria and parainfluenza virus. | Chronic cough. |
| **Distemper** | Disease primarily affecting respiratory and nervous system. | Virus that is related to the human measles virus. | Mild symptoms such as fever, lack of appetite and mucus secretion progress to evidence of brain damage, "hard pad." |
| **Hepatitis** | Virus primarily affecting the liver. | Canine adenovirus type I (CAV-1). Enters system when dog breathes in particles. | Lesser symptoms include listlessness, diarrhea, vomiting. More severe symptoms include "blue-eye" (clumps of virus in eye). |
| **Coronavirus** | Virus resulting in digestive problems. | Virus is spread through infected dog's feces. | Stomach upset evidenced by lack of appetite, vomiting, diarrhea. |

temperament evaluation. At the first visit, your vet will set up your pup's vaccination schedule.

### VACCINATION SCHEDULING

Most vaccinations are given by injection and should only be done by a veterinarian. Both he and you should keep records of the date of the injection, the identification of the vaccine and the amount given. Some vets give a first vaccination at six weeks, but most dog breeders prefer the course not to commence until about eight weeks to avoid negating any antibodies passed on by the dam. The vaccination scheduling is usually based on a 15-day cycle. You must take your vet's advice regarding when to vaccinate, as this may differ according to the vaccine used.

Most vaccinations immunize your puppy against viruses. The usual vaccines contain immunizing doses of several different viruses such as distemper, parvovirus, parainfluenza and hepatitis, although some vets recommend separate vaccines for each disease. There are other vaccines available when the puppy is at risk. You should rely upon professional advice. This is especially true for the booster-shot program. Most vaccination programs require a booster when the puppy is a year old and once a year thereafter. In some cases, circumstances may require more or less frequent immunizations.

Canine cough, more formally known as tracheobronchitis, is treated with a vaccine that is sprayed into the dog's nostrils. Canine cough is usually included in routine vaccination, but this is often not as effective as the vaccines for other major diseases.

### FIVE TO TWELVE MONTHS OF AGE

Unless you intend to breed or show your dog, neutering the puppy around six months of age is recommended. Discuss this with your veterinarian. Neutering and spaying have proven to be extremely beneficial to male and female dogs, respectively. Besides eliminating the possibility of pregnancy and pyometra in bitches and testicular cancer in male dogs, it greatly reduces the risk of breast cancer in bitches and prostate cancer in males.

Your veterinarian should provide your puppy with a thor-

## PUPPY VACCINATIONS

Your veterinarian will probably recommend that your puppy be fully vaccinated before you take him outside. There are airborne diseases, parasite eggs in the grass and unexpected visits from other dogs that might be dangerous to your puppy's health. Other dogs are the most harmful reservoir of pathogenic organisms, as everything they have can be transmitted to your puppy.

# HEALTH AND VACCINATION SCHEDULE

| AGE IN WEEKS: | 6TH | 8TH | 10TH | 12TH | 14TH | 16TH | 20-24TH | 52ND |
|---|---|---|---|---|---|---|---|---|
| Worm Control | ✔ | ✔ | ✔ | ✔ | ✔ | ✔ | ✔ | |
| Neutering | | | | | | | ✔ | |
| Heartworm | | ✔ | | ✔ | | ✔ | ✔ | |
| Parvovirus | ✔ | | ✔ | | ✔ | | ✔ | ✔ |
| Distemper | | ✔ | | ✔ | | ✔ | | ✔ |
| Hepatitis | | ✔ | | ✔ | | ✔ | | ✔ |
| Leptospirosis | | | | | | | | ✔ |
| Parainfluenza | ✔ | | ✔ | | ✔ | | | ✔ |
| Dental Examination | | ✔ | | | | | ✔ | ✔ |
| Complete Physical | | ✔ | | | | | ✔ | ✔ |
| Coronavirus | | | | ✔ | | | ✔ | ✔ |
| Canine Cough | ✔ | | | | | | | |
| Hip Dysplasia | | | | | | | ✔ | |
| Rabies | | | | | | | ✔ | |

Vaccinations are not instantly effective. It takes about two weeks for the dog's immune system to develop antibodies. Most vaccinations require annual booster shots. Your vet should guide you in this regard.

ough dental evaluation at six months of age, ascertaining whether all of the permanent teeth have erupted properly. A home dental-care regimen should be initiated at six months, including brushing weekly and providing good dental devices (such as nylon bones). Regular dental care promotes healthy teeth, fresh breath and a longer life.

### OLDER THAN ONE YEAR
Once a year, your grown dog should visit the vet for an examination and vaccination boosters, if needed. Some vets recommend blood tests, a thyroid-level check and a dental evaluation to accompany these annual visits. A thor-

ough clinical evaluation by the vet can provide critical background information for your dog. Blood tests are often performed at one year of age and then annually. Veterinary tooth-cleaning also may become part of your dog's annual exams. In the long run, quality preventative care for your pet can save money, teeth and lives.

## FOOD PROBLEMS

### FOOD ALLERGIES
Dogs can be allergic to many foods that are best-sellers and highly recommended by breeders and veterinarians. Changing the brand of food that you buy may not eliminate the problem if the

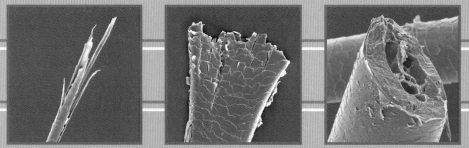

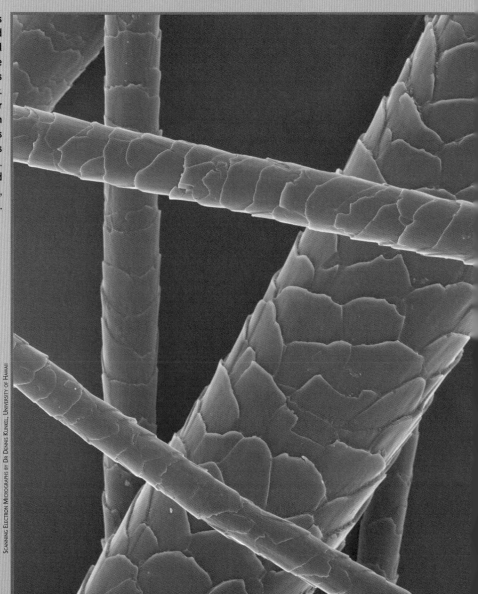

Normal hairs of a dog enlarged 200 times original size. The cuticle (outer covering) is clean and healthy. Unlike human hair that grows from the base, a dog's hair also grows from the end. Damaged hairs and split ends, illustrated above.

element to which the dog is allergic is contained in the new brand.

Recognizing a food allergy is difficult. Humans vomit or have rashes when they eat a food to which they are allergic. Dogs neither vomit nor (usually) develop rashes. They react in the same manner as they would to an airborne or flea allergy; they itch, scratch and bite, thus making the diagnosis extremely difficult. While pollen allergies and parasite bites are usually seasonal, food allergies are year-round problems.

### FOOD INTOLERANCE

Food intolerance is the inability of the dog to completely digest certain foods. For instance, puppies that may have done very well on their mother's milk may not do well on cow's milk. The results of food intolerance may be evident in loose bowels, passing gas and stomach pains. These are the only obvious symptoms of food intolerance, which makes diagnosis difficult.

### TREATING FOOD PROBLEMS

It is possible to handle food allergies and intolerance yourself. Start by putting your dog on a diet that he has never had. Obviously, if the dog has never eaten this new food, he can't yet have been allergic or intolerant of it. Start with a single ingredient that is not in the dog's diet at the present time. Ingredients like chopped beef or chicken are common in dogs' diets, so try

**PROPER DIET**
Feeding your dog properly is very important. An incorrect diet could affect the dog's health, behavior and nervous system, possibly making a normal dog into an aggressive one. Its most visible effects are to the skin and coat, but internal organs are similarly affected.

different source of protein like fish or lamb. Keep the dog on this diet (with no additives) for a month. If the symptoms of food allergy or intolerance disappear, it is quite likely that your dog has a food allergy.

Don't think that the single ingredient cured the problem. You still must find a suitable diet and ascertain which ingredient in the old diet was objectionable. This is most easily done by adding ingredients to the new diet one at a time. Let the dog stay on the modified diet for a month before you add another ingredient. Eventually, you will determine the ingredient that caused the adverse reaction.

An alternative method is to carefully study the ingredients in the diet to which your dog is allergic or intolerant. Identify the main ingredient in this diet and eliminate the main ingredient by buying a different food that does not have that ingredient. Keep experimenting until the symptoms disappear after one month on the new diet.

A male dog flea, *Ctenocephalides canis.*

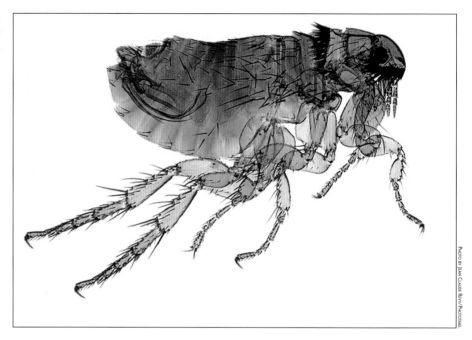

PHOTO BY JEAN CLAUDE REVY/PHOTOTAKE.

## EXTERNAL PARASITES

### FLEAS

Of all the problems to which dogs are prone, none is more well known and frustrating than fleas. Flea infestation is relatively simple to cure but difficult to prevent. Parasites that are harbored inside the body are a bit more difficult to eradicate but they are easier to control.

To control flea infestation, you have to understand the flea's life cycle. Fleas are often thought of as a summertime problem, but centrally heated homes have changed the patterns and fleas can be found at any time of the year. The most effective method of flea control is a two-stage approach: one stage to kill the adult fleas, and the other to control the development of pre-adult fleas. Unfortunately, no single active ingredient is effective against all stages of the life cycle.

### FLEA KILLER CAUTION—"POISON"

Flea-killers are poisonous. You should not spray these toxic chemicals on areas of a dog's body that he licks, including his genitals and his face. Flea killers taken internally are a better answer, but check with your vet in case internal therapy is not advised for your dog.

## LIFE CYCLE STAGES

During its life, a flea will pass through four life stages: egg, larva, pupa or nymph and adult. The adult stage is the most visible and irritating stage of the flea life cycle, and this is why the majority of flea-control products concentrate on this stage. The fact is that adult fleas account for only 1% of the total flea population, and the other 99% exist in pre-adult stages, i.e., eggs, larvae and nymphs. The pre-adult stages are barely visible to the naked eye.

## THE LIFE CYCLE OF THE FLEA

Eggs are laid on the dog, usually in quantities of about 20 or 30, several times a day. The adult female flea must have a blood meal before each egg-laying session. When first laid, the eggs will cling to the dog's hair, as the eggs are still moist. However, they will quickly dry out and fall from the dog, especially if the dog moves around or scratches. Many eggs will fall off in the dog's favorite area or an area in which he spends a lot of time, such as his bed.

Once the eggs fall from the dog onto the carpet or furniture, they will hatch into larvae. This takes from one to ten days. Larvae are not particularly mobile and will usually travel only a few inches from where they hatch. However, they do have a tendency to move away from bright light and heavy

**EN GARDE:
CATCHING FLEAS OFF GUARD!**
Consider the following ways to arm yourself against fleas:
• Add a small amount of pennyroyal or eucalyptus oil to your dog's bath. These natural remedies repel fleas.
• Supplement your dog's food with fresh garlic (minced or grated) and a hearty amount of brewer's yeast, both of which ward off fleas.
• Use a flea comb on your dog daily. Submerge fleas in a cup of bleach to kill them quickly.
• Confine the dog to only a few rooms to limit the spread of fleas in the home.
• Vacuum daily...and get all of the crevices! Dispose of the bag every few days until the problem is under control.
• Wash your dog's bedding daily. Cover cushions where your dog sleeps with towels, and wash the towels often.

traffic—under furniture and behind doors are common places to find high quantities of flea larvae.

The flea larvae feed on dead organic matter, including adult flea feces, until they are ready to change into adult fleas. Fleas will usually remain as larvae for around seven days. After this period, the larvae will pupate into protective pupae. While inside the pupae, the larvae will undergo metamorphosis and change into adult fleas. This can take as little time as a few days, but the adult fleas can remain inside the pupae waiting to hatch for up to two years. The pupae are signaled to hatch by certain stimuli, such as physical pressure—the pupae's being stepped on, heat from an animal's lying on the pupae or increased carbon-dioxide levels and vibrations—indicating that a suitable host is available.

Once hatched, the adult flea must feed within a few days. Once the adult flea finds a host, it will not leave voluntarily. It only becomes dislodged by grooming or the host animal's scratching. The adult flea will remain on the

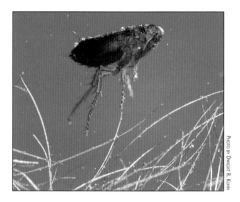

PHOTO BY DWIGHT R. KUHN

host for the duration of its life unless forcibly removed.

### TREATING THE ENVIRONMENT AND THE DOG

Treating fleas should be a two-pronged attack. First, the environment needs to be treated; this includes carpets and furniture, especially the dog's bedding and areas underneath furniture. The environment should be treated with a household spray containing an Insect Growth Regulator (IGR) and an insecticide to kill the adult fleas. Most IGRs are effective against eggs and larvae; they actually mimic the fleas' own hormones and stop the eggs and larvae from developing into adult fleas. There are currently no treatments available to attack the pupa stage of the life cycle, so the adult insecticide is used to kill the newly hatched adult fleas before they find a host. Most IGRs are active for many months, while adult insecticides are only active

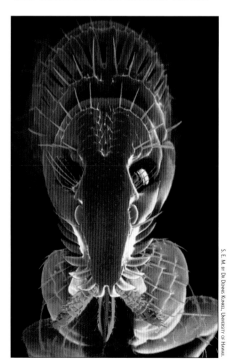

A scanning electron micrograph of a dog or cat flea, *Ctenocephalides*, magnified more than 100x. This image has been colorized for effect.

S. E. M. BY DR DENNIS KUNKEL, UNIVERSITY OF HAWAII.

# THE LIFE CYCLE OF THE FLEA

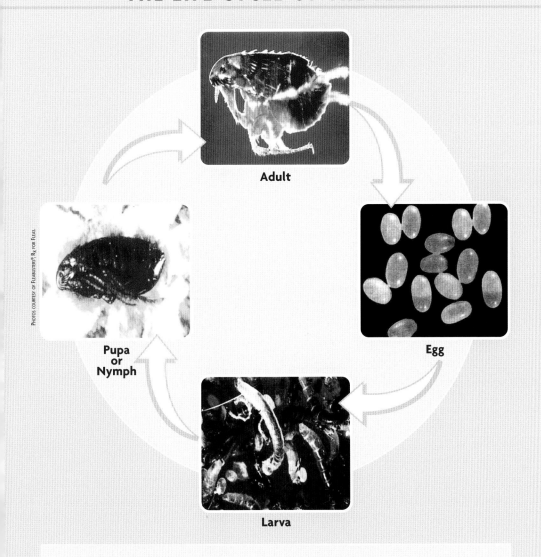

**Adult**

**Egg**

**Larva**

**Pupa or Nymph**

PHOTOS COURTESY OF FLEABUSTERS® Rx FOR FLEAS.

Fleas have been around for millions of years and have adapted to changing host animals. They are able to go through a complete life cycle in less than one month or they can extend their lives to almost two years by remaining as pupae or cocoons. They do not need blood or any other food for up to 20 months.

### INSECT GROWTH REGULATOR (IGR)

Two types of products should be used when treating fleas—a product to treat the pet and a product to treat the home. Adult fleas represent less than 1% of the flea population. The pre-adult fleas (eggs, larvae and pupae) represent more than 99% of the flea population and are found in the environment; it is in the case of pre-adult fleas that products containing an Insect Growth Regulator (IGR) should be used in the home.

IGRs are a new class of compounds used to prevent the development of insects. They do not kill the insect outright, but instead use the insect's biology against it to stop it from completing its growth. Products that contain methoprene are the world's first and leading IGRs. Used to control fleas and other insects, this type of IGR will stop flea larvae from developing and protect the house for up to seven months.

The American dog tick, *Dermacentor variabilis*, is probably the most common tick found on dogs. Look at the strength in its eight legs! No wonder it's hard to detach them.

is to apply an adult insecticide to the dog. Traditionally, this would be in the form of a collar or a spray, but more recent innovations include digestible insecticides that poison the fleas when they ingest the dog's blood. Alternatively, there are drops that, when placed on the back of the dog's neck, spread throughout the hair and skin to kill adult fleas.

### TICKS

Though not as common as fleas, ticks are found all over the tropical and temperate world. They don't bite, like fleas; they harpoon. They dig their sharp proboscis (nose) into the dog's skin and drink the blood. Their only food and drink is dog's for a few days.

When treating with a household spray, it is a good idea to vacuum before applying the product. This stimulates as many pupae as possible to hatch into adult fleas. The vacuum cleaner should also be treated with an insecticide to prevent the eggs and larvae that have been collected in the vacuum bag from hatching.

The second stage of treatment

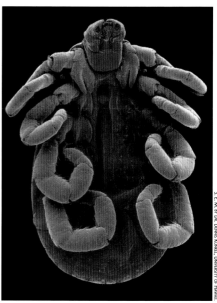

S.E.M. BY DR. DENNIS KUNKEL, UNIVERSITY OF HAWAII

blood. Dogs can get Lyme disease, Rocky Mountain spotted fever, tick bite paralysis and many other diseases from ticks. They may live where fleas are found and they like to hide in cracks or seams in walls. They are controlled the same way fleas are controlled.

The American dog tick, *Dermacentor variabilis*, may well be the most common dog tick in many geographical areas, especially those areas where the climate is hot and humid. Most dog ticks have life expectancies of a week to six months, depending upon climatic conditions. They can neither jump nor fly, but they can crawl slowly and can range up to 16 feet to reach a sleeping or unsuspecting dog.

## MITES

Just as fleas and ticks can be problematic for your dog, mites can also lead to an itchy nuisance. Microscopic in size, mites are related to ticks and generally take up permanent residence on their host animal—in this case, your dog! The term *mange* refers to any infestation caused by one of the mighty mites, of which there are six varieties that concern dog owners.

*Demodex* mites cause a condition known as demodicosis (sometimes called red mange or

**DEER-TICK CROSSING**
The great outdoors may be fun for your dog, but it also is a home to dangerous ticks. Deer ticks carry a bacterium known as *Borrelia burgdorferi* and are most active in the autumn and spring. When infections are caught early, penicillin and tetracycline are effective antibiotics, but, if left untreated, the bacteria may cause neurological, kidney and cardiac problems as well as long-term trouble with walking and painful joints.

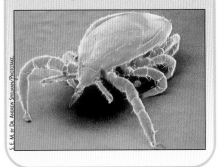

S.E.M. BY DR. ANDREW SPIELMANN/PHOTOTAKE

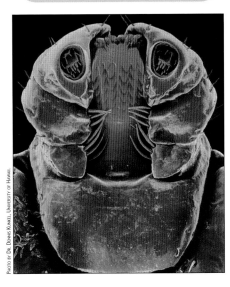

PHOTO BY DR. DENNIS KUNKEL, UNIVERSITY OF HAWAII.

The head of an American dog tick, *Dermacentor variabilis*, enlarged and colorized for effect.

The mange mite, *Psoroptes bovis*, can infest cattle and other domestic animals.

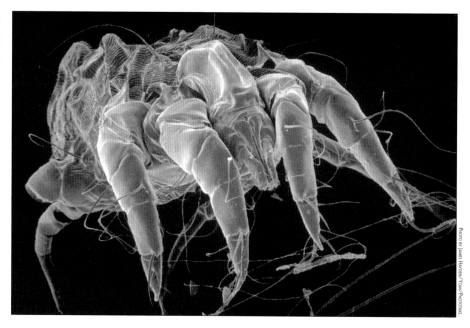

PHOTO BY JAMES HAYDEN/YOAV/PHOTOTAKE.

follicular mange), in which the mites live in the dog's hair follicles and sebaceous glands in larger-than-normal numbers. This type of mange is commonly passed from the dam to her puppies and usually shows up on the puppies' muzzles, though demodicosis is not transferable from one normal dog to another. Most dogs recover from this type of mange without any treatment, though topical therapies are commonly prescribed by the vet.

Human lice look like dog lice; the two are closely related.

PHOTO BY DWIGHT R. KUHN.

The *Cheyletiellosis* mite is the hook-mouthed culprit associated with "walking dandruff," a condition that affects dogs as well as cats and rabbits. This mite lives on the surface of the animal's skin and is readily transferable through direct or indirect contact with an affected animal. The dandruff is present in the form of scaly skin, which may or may not be itchy. If not treated, this mange can affect a whole kennel of dogs and can be spread to humans as well.

The *Sarcoptes* mite causes intense itching on the dog in the form of a condition known as scabies or sarcoptic mange. The cycle of the *Sarcoptes* mite lasts about three weeks, and the mites live in the top layer of the dog's skin (epidermis), preferably in areas with little hair. Scabies is highly contagious and can be passed to humans. Sometimes an allergic reaction to the mite worsens the severe itching associated with sarcoptic mange.

Ear mites, *Otodectes cynotis,* lead to otodectic mange, which most commonly affects the outer ear canal of the dog, though other areas can be affected as well. Dogs with ear-mite infestation commonly scratch at their ears, causing further irritation, and shake their heads. Dark brown droppings in the outer ear confirm the diagnosis. Your vet can prescribe a treatment to flush out the ears and kill any eggs in the ears. A complete month of treatment is necessary to cure the mange.

Two other mites, less common in dogs, include *Dermanyssus gallinae* (the poultry or red mite) and *Eutrombicula alfreddugesi* (the North American mite associated with trombiculidiasis or chigger infestation). The poultry mite frequently lives on chickens, but can transfer to dogs who spend time near farm animals. Chigger infestation affects dogs in the

> **DO NOT MIX**
> Never mix parasite-control products without first consulting your vet. Some products can become toxic when combined with others and can cause fatal consequences.

> **NOT A DROP TO DRINK**
> Never allow your dog to swim in polluted water or public areas where water quality can be suspect. Even perfectly clear water can harbor parasites, many of which can cause serious to fatal illnesses in canines. Areas inhabited by waterfowl and other wildlife are especially dangerous.

central US who have exposure to woodlands. The types of mange caused by both of these mites are treatable by vets.

**INTERNAL PARASITES**

Most animals—fishes, birds and mammals, including dogs and humans—have worms and other parasites that live inside their bodies. According to Dr. Herbert R. Axelrod, the fish pathologist, there are two kinds of parasites: dumb and smart. The smart parasites live in peaceful cooperation with their hosts (symbiosis), while the dumb parasites kill their hosts. Most worm infections are relatively easy to control. If they are not controlled, they weaken the host dog to the point that other medical problems occur, but they do not kill the host as dumb parasites would.

A brown dog tick, *Rhipicephalus sanguineus*, is an uncommon but annoying tick found on dogs.

Photo by Carolina Biological Supply/Phototake

The roundworm *Rhabditis* can infect both dogs and humans.

## ROUNDWORMS

Average-size dogs can pass 1,360,000 roundworm eggs every day. For example, if there were only 1 million dogs in the world, the world would be saturated with thousands of tons of dog feces. These feces would contain around 15,000,000,000 roundworm eggs.

Up to 31% of home yards and children's sand boxes in the US contain roundworm eggs.

Flushing dog's feces down the toilet is not a safe practice because the usual sewage treatments do not destroy roundworm eggs.

Infected puppies start shedding roundworm eggs at three weeks of age. They can be infected by their mother's milk.

The roundworm, *Ascaris lumbricoides.*

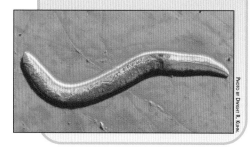

Photo by Dwight R. Kuhn.

## ROUNDWORMS

The roundworms that infect dogs are known scientifically as *Toxocara canis*. They live in the dog's intestines and shed eggs continually. It has been estimated that a dog produces about 6 or more ounces of feces every day. Each ounce of feces averages hundreds of thousands of roundworm eggs. There are no known areas in which dogs roam that do not contain roundworm eggs. The greatest danger of roundworms is that they infect people, too! It is wise to have your dog tested regularly for roundworms.

In young puppies, roundworms cause bloated bellies, diarrhea, coughing and vomiting, and are transmitted from the dam (through blood or milk). Affected puppies will not appear as animated as normal puppies. The worms appear spaghetti-like, measuring as long as 6 inches. Adult dogs can acquire roundworms through coprophagia (eating contaminated feces) or by killing rodents that carry roundworms.

Roundworm infection can kill puppies and cause severe problems in adults, as the hatched larvae travel to the lungs and trachea through the bloodstream. Cleanliness is the best preventative for roundworms. Always pick up after your dog and dispose of feces in appropriate receptacles.

PHOTO BY DWIGHT R. KUHN.

The hookworm, *Ancylostoma caninum.*

## HOOKWORMS

In the United States, dog owners have to be concerned about four different species of hookworm, the most common and most serious of which is *Ancylostoma caninum*, which prefers warm climates. The others are *Ancylostoma braziliense, Ancylostoma tubaeforme* and *Uncinaria stenocephala*, the latter of which is a concern to dogs living in the northern US and Canada, as this species prefers cold climates.

Hookworms are dangerous to humans as well as to dogs and cats, and can be the cause of severe anemia due to iron deficiency. The worm uses its teeth to attach itself to the dog's intestines and changes the site of its attachment about six times per day. Each time the worm repositions itself, the dog loses blood and can become anemic. *Ancylostoma caninum* is the most likely of the four species to cause anemia in the dog.

Symptoms of hookworm infection include dark stools, weight loss, general weakness, pale coloration and anemia, as well as possible skin problems. Fortunately, hookworms are easily purged from the affected dog with a number of medications that have proven effective. Discuss these with your vet. Most heartworm preventatives include a hookworm insecticide as well.

Owners also must be aware that hookworms can infect humans, who can acquire the larvae through exposure to contaminated feces. Since the worms cannot complete their life cycle on a human, the worms simply infest the skin and cause irritation. This condition is known as cutaneous larva migrans syndrome. As a preventative, use disposable gloves or a "poop-scoop" to pick up your dog's droppings and prevent your dog (or neighborhood cats) from defecating in children's play areas.

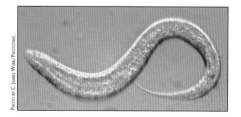

PHOTO BY C. JAMES WEBB/PHOTOTAKE.

The infective stage of the hookworm larva.

## TAPEWORMS

Humans, rats, squirrels, foxes, coyotes, wolves and domestic dogs are all susceptible to tapeworm infection. Except in humans, tapeworms are usually not a fatal infection. Infected individuals can harbor 1000 parasitic worms.

Tapeworms, like some other types of worm, are hermaphroditic, meaning male and female in the same worm.

If dogs eat infected rats or mice, or anything else infected with tapeworm, they get the tapeworm disease. One month after attaching to a dog's intestine, the worm starts shedding eggs. These eggs are infective immediately. Infective eggs can live for a few months without a host animal.

The head and rostellum (the round prominence on the scolex) of a tapeworm, which infects dogs and humans.

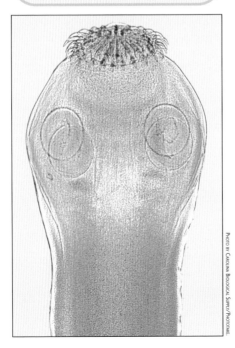

PHOTO BY CAROLINA BIOLOGICAL SUPPLY/PHOTOTAKE

## TAPEWORMS

There are many species of tapeworm, all of which are carried by fleas! The most common tapeworm affecting dogs is known as *Dipylidium caninum*. The dog eats the flea and starts the tapeworm cycle. Humans can also be infected with tapeworms—so don't eat fleas! Fleas are so small that your dog could pass them onto your hands, your plate or your food and thus make it possible for you to ingest a flea that is carrying tapeworm eggs.

While tapeworm infection is not life-threatening in dogs (smart parasite!), it can be the cause of a very serious liver disease for humans. About 50% of the humans infected with *Echinococcus multilocularis*, a type of tapeworm that causes alveolar hydatid, perish.

## WHIPWORMS

In North America, whipworms are counted among the most common parasitic worms in dogs. The whipworm's scientific name is *Trichuris vulpis*. These worms attach themselves in the lower parts of the intestine, where they feed. Affected dogs may only experience upset tummies, colic and diarrhea. These worms, however, can live for months or years in the dog, beginning their larval stage in the small intestine, spending their adult stage in the large intestine and finally passing infective eggs through the dog's feces. The only way to detect whipworms is through a fecal examination, though this is not always foolproof. Treatment for whipworms is tricky, due to the worms' unusual life-cycle pattern, and very often dogs are reinfected due to exposure to infective eggs on the ground. The whipworm eggs can survive in the environment for as long as five years; thus, cleaning up droppings in your own backyard as well as in public places is absolutely essential for sanitation purposes and the health of your dog and others.

### THREADWORMS

Though less common than round-worms, hookworms and those previously mentioned, thread-worms concern dog owners in the southwestern US and Gulf Coast area where the climate is hot and humid. Living in the small intestine of the dog, this worm measures a mere 2 millimeters and is round in shape. Like that of the whipworm, the threadworm's life cycle is very complex and the eggs and larvae are passed through the feces. A deadly disease in humans, *Strongyloides* readily infects people, and the handling of feces is the most common means of transmission. Threadworms are most often seen in young puppies; bloody diarrhea and pneumonia are symptoms. Sick puppies must be isolated and treated immediately; vets recommend a follow-up treatment one month later.

## HEARTWORM PREVENTATIVES

There are many heartworm preventatives on the market, many of which are sold at your veterinarian's office. These products can be given daily or monthly, depending on the manufacturer's instructions. All of these preventatives contain chemical insecticides directed at killing heartworms, which leads to some controversy among dog owners. In effect, heartworm preventatives are necessary evils, though you should determine how necessary based on your pet's lifestyle. There is no doubt that heartworm is a dreadful disease that threatens the lives of dogs. However, the likelihood of your dog's being bitten by an infected mosquito is slim in most places, and a mosquito-repellent (or an herbal remedy such as Wormwood or Black Walnut) is much safer for your dog and will not compromise his immune system (the way heartworm preventatives will). Should you decide to use the traditional preventative "medications," you can consider giving the pill every other or third month. Since the toxins in the pill will kill the heartworms at all stages of development, the pill would be effective in killing larvae, nymphs or adults, and it takes four months for the larvae to reach the adult stage. Thus, there is no rationale to poisoning the dog's system on a monthly basis. Lastly, do not give the pill during the winter months since there are no mosquitoes around to pass on their infection, unless you live in a tropical environment.

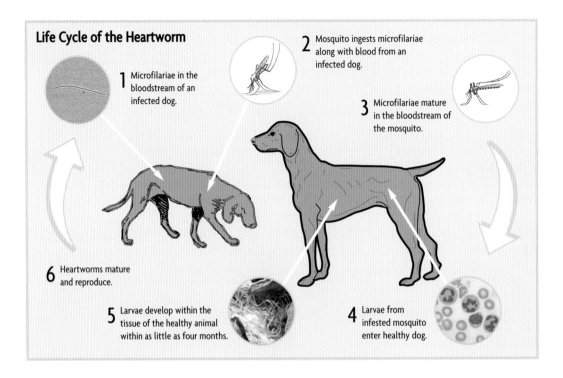

**Life Cycle of the Heartworm**

1 Microfilariae in the bloodstream of an infected dog.

2 Mosquito ingests microfilariae along with blood from an infected dog.

3 Microfilariae mature in the bloodstream of the mosquito.

6 Heartworms mature and reproduce.

5 Larvae develop within the tissue of the healthy animal within as little as four months.

4 Larvae from infested mosquito enter healthy dog.

### HEARTWORMS

Heartworms are thin, extended worms up to 12 inches long, which live in a dog's heart and the major blood vessels surrounding it. Dogs may have up to 200 worms. Symptoms may be loss of energy, loss of appetite, coughing, the development of a pot belly and anemia.

Heartworms are transmitted by mosquitoes. The mosquito drinks the blood of an infected dog and takes in larvae with the blood. The larvae, called microfilariae, develop within the body of the mosquito and are passed on to the next dog bitten after the larvae mature. It takes two to three weeks for the larvae to develop to the infective stage within the body of the mosquito. Dogs are usually treated at about six weeks of age and maintained on a prophylactic dose given monthly.

Blood testing for heartworms is not necessarily indicative of how seriously your dog is infected. Although this is a dangerous disease, it is not easy for a dog to be infected. Discuss the various preventatives with your vet, as there are many different types now available. Together you can decide on a safe course of prevention for your dog.

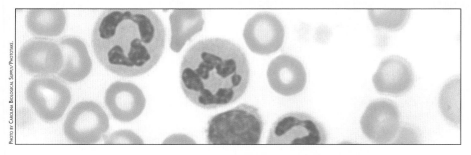

Magnified heartworm larvae, *Dirofilaria immitis.*

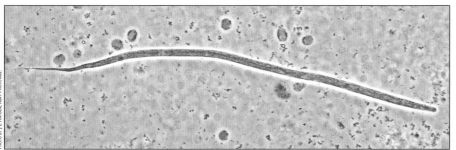

Heartworm, *Dirofilaria immitis.*

The heart of a dog infected with canine heartworm, *Dirofilaria immitis.*

# HOMEOPATHY:
an alternative
to conventional
medicine

## "Less is Most"

Using this principle, the strength of a homeopathic remedy is measured by the number of serial dilutions that were undertaken to create it. The greater the number of serial dilutions, the greater the strength of the homeopathic remedy. The potency of a remedy that has been made by making a dilution of 1 part in 100 parts (or 1/100) is 1c or 1cH. If this remedy is subjected to a series of further dilutions, each one being 1/100, a more dilute and stronger remedy is produced. If the remedy is diluted in this way six times, it is called 6c or 6cH. A dilution of 6c is 1 part in 1,000,000,000,000. In general, higher potencies in more frequent doses are better for acute symptoms and lower potencies in more infrequent doses are more useful for chronic, long-standing problems.

## CURING OUR DOGS NATURALLY

Holistic medicine means treating the whole animal as a unique, perfect, living being. Generally, holistic treatments do not suppress the symptoms that the body naturally produces, as do most medications prescribed by conventional doctors and vets. Holistic methods seek to cure disease by regaining balance and harmony in the patient's environment. Some of these methods include use of nutritional therapy, herbs, flower essences, aromatherapy, acupuncture, massage, chiropractic and, of course, the most popular holistic approach, homeopathy.

Homeopathy is a theory or system of treating illness with small doses of substances which, if administered in larger quantities, would produce the symptoms that the patient already has. This approach is often described as "like cures like." Although modern veterinary medicine is geared toward the "quick fix," homeopathy relies on the belief that, given the time, the body is able to heal itself and return to its natural, healthy state.

Choosing a remedy to cure a problem in our dogs is the difficult part of homeopathy. Consult with your vet for a professional diagnosis of your dog's symptoms. Often these symptoms require immediate conventional care. If your vet is willing and knowledgeable, you may attempt a homeopathic remedy. Be aware that cortisone prevents homeopathic remedies from working. There are hundreds of possibilities and combinations to cure many problems in dogs, from basic physical problems such as excessive shedding, fleas or other parasites, unattractive doggy odor, bad breath, upset tummy, obesity, dry, oily or dull coat, diarrhea, ear problems or eye discharge (including tears and dry or mucousy matter), to behavioral abnormalities such as fear of loud noises, habitual licking, poor appetite, excessive barking and various phobias. From alumina to zincum metallicum, the remedies span the planet and the imagination…from flowers and weeds to chemicals, insect droppings, diesel smoke and volcanic ash.

# Using "Like to Treat Like"

Unlike conventional medicines that suppress symptoms, homeopathic remedies treat illnesses with small doses of substances that, if administered in larger quantities, would produce the symptoms that the patient already has. While the same homeopathic remedy can be used to treat different symptoms in different dogs, here are some interesting remedies and their uses.

### Apis Mellifica
(made from honey bee venom) can be used for allergies or to reduce swelling that occurs in acutely infected kidneys.

### Diesel Smoke
can be used to help control travel sickness.

### Calcarea Fluorica
(made from calcium fluoride, which helps harden bone structure) can be useful in treating hard lumps in tissues.

### Natrum Muriaticum
(made from common salt, sodium chloride) is useful in treating thin, thirsty dogs.

### Nitricum Acidum
(made from nitric acid) is used for symptoms you would expect to see from contact with acids, such as lesions, especially where the skin joins the linings of body orifices or openings such as the lips and nostrils.

### Symphytum
(made from the herb Knitbone, *Symphytum officianale*) is used to encourage bones to heal.

### Urtica Urens
(made from the common stinging nettle) is used in treating painful, irritating rashes.

# First Aid at a Glance

### Burns
Place the affected area under cool water; use ice if only a small area is burnt.

### Bee stings/Insect bites
Apply ice to relieve swelling; antihistamine dosed properly.

### Animal bites
Clean any bleeding area; apply pressure until bleeding subsides; go to the vet.

### Spider bites
Use cold compress and a pressurized pack to inhibit venom's spreading.

### Antifreeze poisoning
Induce vomiting with hydrogen peroxide. Seek *immediate* veterinary help!

### Fish hooks
Removal best handled by vet; hook must be cut in order to remove.

### Snake bites
Pack ice around bite; contact vet quickly; identify snake for proper antivenin.

### Car accident
Move dog from roadway with blanket; seek veterinary aid.

### Shock
Calm the dog; keep him warm; seek immediate veterinary help.

### Nosebleed
Apply cold compress to the nose; apply pressure to any visible abrasion.

### Bleeding
Apply pressure above the area; treat wound by applying a cotton pack.

### Heat stroke
Submerge dog in cold bath; cool down with fresh air and water; go to the vet.

### Frostbite/Hypothermia
Warm the dog with a warm bath, electric blankets or hot water bottles.

### Abrasions
Clean the wound and wash out thoroughly with fresh water; apply antiseptic.

 *Remember: an injured dog may attempt to bite a helping hand from fear and confusion. Always muzzle the dog before trying to offer assistance.*

## Recognizing a Sick Dog

Unlike colicky babies and cranky children, our canine kids cannot tell us when they are feeling ill. Therefore, there are a number of signs that owners can identify to know that their dogs are not feeling well.

**Take note for
physical manifestations such as:**

- unusual, bad odor, including bad breath
- excessive shedding
- wax in the ears, chronic ear irritation
- oily, flaky, dull haircoat
- mucus, tearing or similar discharge in the eyes
- fleas or mites
- mucus in stool, diarrhea
- sensitivity to petting or handling
- licking at paws, scratching face, etc.

**Keep an eye out for
behavioral changes as well, including:**

- lethargy, idleness
- lack of patience or general irritability
- lack of interest in food
- phobias (fear of people, loud noises, etc.)
- strange behavior, suspicion, fear
- coprophagia
- more frequent barking
- whimpering, crying

## Get Well Soon

You don't need a DVM to provide good TLC to your sick or recovering dog, but you do need to pay attention to some details that normally wouldn't bother him. The following tips will aid Fido's recovery and get him back on his paws again:

- Keep his space free of irritating smells, like heavy perfumes and air fresheners.
- Rest is the best medicine! Avoid harsh lighting that will prevent your dog from sleeping. Shade him from bright sunlight during the day and dim the lights in the evening.
- Keep the noise level down. Animals are more sensitive to sound when they are sick.

- Be attentive to any necessary temperature adjustments. A dog with a fever needs a cool room and cold liquids. A bitch that is whelping or recovering from surgery will be more comfortable in a warm room, consuming warm liquids and food.
- You wouldn't send a sick child back to school early, so don't rush your dog back into a full routine until he seems absolutely ready.

# Number-One Killer Disease in Dogs: CANCER

In every age, there is a word associated with a disease or plague that causes humans to shudder. In the 21st century, that word is "cancer." Just as cancer is the leading cause of death in humans, it claims nearly half the lives of dogs that die from a natural disease as well as half the dogs that die over the age of ten years.

Described as a genetic disease, cancer becomes a greater risk as the dog ages. Vets and dog owners have become increasingly aware of the threat of cancer to dogs. Statistics reveal that one dog in every five will develop cancer, the most common of which is skin cancer. Many cancers, including prostate, ovarian and breast cancer, can be avoided by spaying and neutering our dogs by the age of six months.

Early detection of cancer can save or extend a dog's life, so it is absolutely vital for owners to have their dogs examined by a qualified vet or oncologist immediately upon detection of any abnormality. Certain dietary guidelines have also proven to reduce the onset and spread of cancer. Foods based on fish rather than beef, due to the presence of Omega-3 fatty acids, are recommended. Other amino acids such as glutamine have significant benefits for canines, particularly those breeds that show a greater susceptibility to cancer.

Cancer management and treatments promise hope for future generations of canines. Since the disease is genetic, breeders should never breed a dog whose parents, grandparents and any related siblings have developed cancer. It is difficult to know whether to exclude an otherwise healthy dog from a breeding program, as the disease does not manifest itself until the dog's senior years.

## RECOGNIZE CANCER WARNING SIGNS

Since early detection can possibly rescue your dog from becoming a cancer statistic, it is essential for owners to recognize the possible signs and seek the assistance of a qualified professional.

- Abnormal bumps or lumps that continue to grow
- Bleeding or discharge from any body cavity
- Persistent stiffness or lameness
- Recurrent sores or sores that do not heal
- Inappetence
- Breathing difficulties
- Weight loss
- Bad breath or odors
- General malaise and fatigue
- Eating and swallowing problems
- Difficulty urinating and defecating

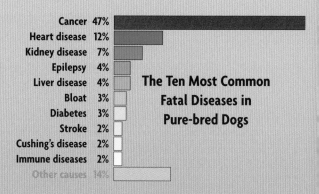

| Disease | % |
|---|---|
| Cancer | 47% |
| Heart disease | 12% |
| Kidney disease | 7% |
| Epilepsy | 4% |
| Liver disease | 4% |
| Bloat | 3% |
| Diabetes | 3% |
| Stroke | 2% |
| Cushing's disease | 2% |
| Immune diseases | 2% |
| Other causes | 14% |

**The Ten Most Common Fatal Diseases in Pure-bred Dogs**

# CDS: COGNITIVE DYSFUNCTION SYNDROME
## "Old-Dog Syndrome"

There are many ways for you to evaluate old-dog syndrome. Veterinarians have defined CDS (cognitive dysfunction syndrome) as the gradual deterioration of cognitive abilities. These are indicated by changes in the dog's behavior. When a dog changes his routine response, and maladies have been eliminated as the cause of these behavioral changes, then CDS is the usual diagnosis.

More than half the dogs over eight years old suffer from some form of CDS. The older the dog, the more chance he has of suffering from CDS. In humans, doctors often dismiss the CDS behavioral changes as part of "winding down."

There are four major signs of CDS: frequent potty accidents inside the home, sleeping much more or much less than normal, acting confused and failing to respond to social stimuli.

## SYMPTOMS OF CDS

### FREQUENT POTTY ACCIDENTS
- *Urinates in the house.*
- *Defecates in the house.*
- *Doesn't signal that he wants to go out.*

### SLEEP PATTERNS
- *Awakens more slowly.*
- *Sleeps more than normal during the day.*
- *Sleeps less during the night.*

### CONFUSION
- *Goes outside and just stands there.*
- *Appears confused with a faraway look in his eyes.*
- *Hides more often.*
- *Doesn't recognize friends.*
- *Doesn't come when called.*
- *Walks around listlessly and without a destination.*

### FAILURE TO RESPOND TO SOCIAL STIMULI
- *Comes to people less frequently, whether called or not.*
- *Doesn't tolerate petting for more than a short time.*
- *Doesn't come to the door when you return home.*

# YOUR SENIOR

# BERGAMASCO

The term *old* is a qualitative term. For dogs, as well as for their masters, old is relative. Certainly we can all distinguish between a puppy Bergamasco and an adult Bergamasco—there are the obvious physical traits, such as size, coat development and facial expressions, and personality traits. Puppies and young dogs like to play with children. Children's natural exuberance is a good match for the seemingly endless energy of young dogs. They like to run, jump, chase and retrieve. When dogs grow older and cease their interaction with children, they are often thought of as being too old to keep pace with the children. On the other hand, if a Bergamasco is only exposed to older people or quieter lifestyles, his life will normally be less active and the decrease in his activity level as he ages will not be as obvious.

If people live to be 100 years old, dogs live to be 20 years old. While this might seem like a viable rule of thumb, it is *very* inaccurate. When trying to compare dog years to human years, you cannot make a general-ization about all dogs. You can make the generalization that 14 years is a good lifespan for a Bergamasco. This breed is considered physically mature as late as three or four years age, but, of course, can reproduce much earlier. Generally speaking, it is more accurate to say that the first three years of a dog's life are like seven times that of comparable humans. That means a 3-year-old dog is like a 21-year-old human. As the curve of comparison shows, however, there is no hard

## CONSISTENCY COUNTS
Puppies and older dogs are very similar in their need for consistency in their lives. Older pets may experience hearing and vision loss, or may just be more easily confused by changes in their homes. Try to keep things consistent for the senior dog. For example, doors that are always open or closed should remain so. Most importantly, don't dismiss a pet just because he's getting old; most senior dogs remain active and important parts of their owners' lives.

and fast rule for comparing dog and human ages. Small breeds tend to live longer than large breeds; some breeds' adolescent periods last longer than others' and some breeds experience rapid periods of growth. The comparison is made even more difficult, for, likewise, not all humans age at the same rate.

## WHAT TO LOOK FOR IN SENIORS

Most veterinarians and behaviorists use the seven-year mark as the time to consider a dog a "senior." This term does not imply that the dog is geriatric and has begun to fail in mind and body. Aging is essentially a slowing process. Humans readily admit that they feel a difference in their activity level from age 20 to 30, and then from 30 to 40, etc. By treating the seven-year-old dog as a senior, owners are able to implement certain therapeutic and preventative medical strategies with the help of their veterinarians. A senior-care program should include at least two veterinary visits per year and screening sessions to determine the dog's health status, as well as nutritional counseling. Vets determine the senior dog's health status through a blood smear for a complete blood count, serum chemistry profile with electrolytes, urinalysis, blood pressure check, electrocar-

diogram, ocular tonometry (pressure on the eyeball) and dental prophylaxis.

Such an extensive program for senior dogs is well advised before owners start to see the obvious physical signs of aging, such as slower and inhibited movement, graying, increased sleep/nap periods and disinterest in play and other activity. This preventative program promises a longer, healthier life for the aging dog. Among the physical problems common in aging dogs are the loss of sight and hearing, arthritis, kidney and liver failure, diabetes mellitus, heart disease and Cushing's disease (a hormonal disease).

In addition to the physical manifestations discussed, there are some behavioral changes and problems related to aging dogs. Dogs suffering from hearing or

The senior Bergamasco becomes less active and requires considerably less exercise along with appropriate dietary changes.

vision loss, dental discomfort or arthritis can become aggressive. Likewise, the near-deaf and/or blind dog may be startled more easily and react in an unexpect-edly aggressive manner. Seniors suffering from senility can become more impatient and irritable. Housesoiling accidents are associated with loss of mobility, kidney problems and loss of sphincter control as well as plaque accumulation, physio-logical brain changes and reactions to medications. Older dogs, just like young puppies, can suffer from separation anxiety, which can lead to excessive barking, whining, housesoiling and destructive behavior. Seniors may become fearful of everyday sounds, such as vacuum cleaners, heaters, thunder and passing traffic. Some dogs have difficulty sleeping, due to discomfort, the need for frequent toilet visits and the like.

Owners should avoid spoiling the older dog with too many treats. Obesity is a common problem in older dogs and subtracts years from their lives. Keep the senior dog as trim as possible, since excess weight puts additional stress on the body's vital organs. Some breeders recommend supplementing the diet with foods high in fiber and lower in calories. Adding fresh vegetables and marrow broth to the senior's diet makes a tasty,

low-calorie, low-fat supplement. Vets also offer specialty diets for senior dogs that are worth exploring.

Your dog, as he nears his twilight years, needs your patience and good care more than ever. Never punish an older dog for an accident or abnormal behavior. For all the years of love, protection and companionship that your dog has provided, he deserves special attention and courtesies. The older dog may need to relieve himself at 3 a.m. because he can no longer "hold it" for eight hours. Older dogs may not be able to remain crated for more than two or three hours. It may be time to give up a sofa or chair to your old friend. Although he may not seem as enthusiastic about your attention and petting, he does appreciate the considera-tions you offer as he gets older.

Your Bergamasco does not understand why his world is slowing down. Owners must make their dogs' transition into their golden years as pleasant and rewarding as possible.

**WHEN THE TIME COMES**
You are never fully prepared to make a rational decision about putting your dog to sleep. It is very obvious that you love your Bergamasco or you would not be reading this book. Putting a beloved dog to sleep is extremely difficult. It is a decision that must

 **TALK IT OUT**

The more openly your family discusses the whole stressful occurrence of the aging and eventual loss of a beloved pet, the easier it will be for you when the time comes.

**WHAT IS EUTHANASIA?**

Euthanasia derives from the Greek, meaning *good death*. In other words, it means the planned, painless killing of a dog suffering from a painful, incurable condition, or who is so aged that he cannot walk, see, eat or control his excretory functions. Euthanasia is usually accomplished by injection with an overdose of anesthesia or a barbiturate. Aside from the prick of the needle, the experience is usually painless.

**MAKING THE DECISION**

The decision to euthanize your dog is never easy. The days during which the dog becomes ill and the end occurs can be unusually stressful for you. If this is your first experience with the death of a loved one, you

be made with your veterinarian. You are usually forced to make the decision when your dog experiences one or more life-threatening symptoms, requiring you to seek veterinary help.

If the prognosis of the malady indicates that the end is near and that your beloved pet will only continue to suffer and experience no enjoyment for the balance of his life, then euthanasia is the right choice.

Your vet can help you locate a reputable pet cemetery if you choose to memorialize your beloved dog in this way.

may need the comfort dictated by your religious beliefs. If you are the head of the family and have children, you should have involved them in the decision of putting your Bergamasco to sleep. Usually your dog can be maintained on drugs at the vet's clinic for a few days in order to give you ample time to make a decision. During this time, talking with members of your family, religious representatives or people who have lived through the same experience can ease the burden of your inevitable decision.

### THE FINAL RESTING PLACE

Dogs can have some of the same privileges as humans. The remains of your beloved dog can be buried in a pet cemetery, which is generally expensive. A dog who has died at home can be buried in your yard in a place suitably marked with a special stone or a newly planted tree or bush. Alternatively, your dog can be cremated individually and the ashes returned to you. A less expensive option is mass cremation, although, of course, the ashes of individual dogs cannot then be returned. Vets can usually arrange the cremation on your behalf or help you locate a pet cemetery if you choose one of these options. The cost of these options should always be discussed frankly and openly with your veterinarian.

### GETTING ANOTHER DOG?

The grief of losing your beloved dog will be as lasting as the grief of losing a human friend or relative. In most cases, if your dog died of old age (if there is such a thing), he had slowed down considerably. Do you now want a new Bergamasco puppy? Or are you better off finding a more mature Bergamasco, say two to three years of age, which will usually be house-trained and will have an already developed personality. In this case, you can find out if you like each other after a few hours of being together.

The decision is, of course, your own. Do you want another dog or perhaps a different breed so as to avoid comparison with your beloved friend? Most people usually choose the same breed because they know and love the characteristics of that breed. Then, too, they often know people who have the same breed and perhaps they are lucky enough that a breeder they know and respect expects a litter soon.

# SHOWING YOUR

# BERGAMASCO

It is always a joy to watch the Bergamasco's gentle unhurried trot and fluid motion as he ambles around the show ring. The flocks of an adult Bergamasco flop and flow from side to side—poetry in motion. You usually hear excited inquiries from the unknowing spectators: "What is that dog?" "Where does he come from?"

There are a few basic guidelines to help you show your Bergamasco properly. Conformation classes should begin when your Bergamasco is just a puppy.

Show conformation training should be enjoyable and neither particularly strict nor monotonous. Classes are for both you and the puppy. It is a good time to spend together and you both will learn. The puppy will probably learn what is necessary for the ring faster than you will learn how to show your puppy. The more you attempt to show and the more classes in which you partake, the easier show handling will become. Showing is a joint effort between you and your Bergamasco. Remember that your dog is only as good as his handler, provided the dog is willing and you are able. If you are unable to attend classes, there are many videos and books that can help as well.

When participating in a show with your dog, the rule of thumb is to have your apparel complement your dog's coat color. The two of you must look like a finished picture. Contrasting clothing colors should help to accent and show off your dog more easily. Proper dress should be worn when showing your dog; it is not advisable to wear informal clothing in the ring. Handling

## CLUB CONTACTS

You can get information about dog shows from kennel clubs and breed clubs:

Fédération Cynologique Internationale
14, rue Leopold II, B-6530 Thuin, Belgium
www.fci.be

American Rare Breed Association
9921 Frank Tippett Road
Cheltenham, MD 20623
www.arba.org

The Kennel Club
1-5 Clarges St., Piccadilly,
London W1Y 8AB, UK
www.the-kennel-club.org.uk

class will teach the basics of "stacking" (the proper way to set up your dog when he's standing), gaiting (the proper way to move yourself and your dog in the ring, including the patterns that the judge may request) and the way to make your dog look his best at all times.

Handling class will help with the use of a proper show collar and lead. There are many varieties of show leads and collars; however, I find that the thin four-foot leather lead works the best without slipping through your fingers. Don't be afraid to ask someone with more experience to give you some advice. Practice makes for Best in Show! When in the ring working together as a team, you and your Bergamasco will develop an even closer camaraderie.

Over the years, many similar working breeds have changed from their original appearance to accommodate personal whims. It

*Showing classes will prepare an owner for handling the Bergamasco in conformation shows, which includes training the dog to "stack" properly.*

**SHOW-QUALITY SHOWS**
While you may purchase a puppy in the hope of having a successful career in the show ring, it is impossible to tell, at twelve or so weeks of age, whether your dog will be a contender. Some promising pups end up with minor to serious faults that prevent them from taking home an award, but this certainly does not mean they can't be the best of companions for you and your family. To find out if your potential show dog is show-quality, enter him in a match to see how a judge evaluates him. You may also take him back to your breeder as he matures to see what he might advise.

is important to remember that the Bergamasco's appearance has remained much the same for hundreds of years, and we do not want to change the Bergamasco's natural looks or elegant demeanor. It is not necessary to bathe the Bergamasco for every show event, which is commonly done for most other breeds. Any visible dirt or odor can be removed by brushing or by giving a simple spot bath. The mouth and under the chin should be clean of any food debris and the coat should be brushed to tidy up the hair. Even though dog shows have become quite competitive these days, we must remember

our Bergamascos' origins and never take away these characteristics from our herding/flock guard.

## CONFORMATION SHOWS

A conformation show is another term for a dog show. The term "conformation" derives from the notion that the dog must "conform" to the breed standard. Firstly, you must understand that the dogs are not actually compared against one another. The judge compares each dog against his breed standard, which is a written description of the ideal specimen of the breed. While some early breed standards were indeed based on specific dogs that were famous or popular, many dedicated enthusiasts say that a perfect specimen, as described in the standard, has never walked into a show ring, has never been bred and, to the woe of dog breeders around the globe, does not exist. Breeders

The Bergamasco puppy may be judged on a table, so it's advisable to acclimate the pup to standing on a table during grooming sessions.

attempt to get as close to this ideal as possible with every litter, but theoretically the "perfect" dog is so elusive that it is impossible. (And if the "perfect" dog were born, breeders and judges would never agree that it was indeed "perfect.")

The second concept that the canine novice learns when watching a dog show is that each dog first competes against members of his own breed. Once the judge has selected the best member of each breed (Best of Breed), provided that the show is judged on a Group system, that chosen dog will compete with other dogs in his group. Finally, the best of each group will compete for Best in Show.

If you are interested in exploring the world of dog showing, your best bet is to join your local breed club. These clubs often host shows, match meetings

### NEATNESS COUNTS

Surely you've spent hours grooming your dog to perfection for the show ring, but don't forget about yourself! While the dog should be the center of attention, it is important that you also appear neat and clean. Wear smart, appropriate clothes and comfortable shoes in a color that contrasts with your dog's coat. Look and act like a professional.

and special events, all of which could be of interest, even if you are only an onlooker. Clubs also send out newsletters, and some organize training days and seminars in order that people may learn more about their chosen breed. To locate the breed club closest to you, check online or contact your dog's registry. You may want to look into not only conformation shows but also working trials, agility trials and obedience shows. Your registry furnishes the rules and regulations for all of these events plus general dog registration and other basic requirements of dog ownership.

Virtually all countries with a recognized specialty breed club (sometimes called a "parent" club) offer show conformation

**PRACTICE AT HOME**
If you have decided to show your dog, you must train him to gait around the ring by your side at the correct pace and pattern, and to tolerate being handled and examined by the judge. Most breeds require complete dentition, all breeds require a particular bite (scissors, level or undershot) and all males must have two apparently normal testicles fully descended into the scrotum. Enlist family and friends to hold mock trials in your yard to prepare your future champion!

competition specifically for and among Bergamascos. Under direction of the club, other special events for herding, tracking, obedience and agility may be offered as well, whether for titling or just for fun.

**OBEDIENCE TRIALS**
Obedience trials in the US trace back to the early 1930s when organized obedience training was developed to demonstrate how well dog and owner could work together. The pioneer of obedience trials is Mrs. Helen Whitehouse Walker, a Standard Poodle fancier, who designed a series of exercises after the Associated Sheep, Police, Army Dog Society of Great Britain. Since the days of Mrs. Walker, obedience trials have grown by leaps and bounds, and today there are over 2,000 trials held in the US every year, with more than 100,000 dogs competing. Any registered dog can enter an obedience trial, regardless of conformational disqualifications or neutering. To give readers an idea of how obedience is organized, we will discuss AKC obedience here.

Obedience trials are divided into three levels of progressive difficulty. At the first level, the Novice, dogs compete for the title Companion Dog (CD); at the intermediate level, the Open, dogs compete for the title Companion Dog Excellent (CDX); and at the

Show-quality Bergamascos are unmistakable. This handsome group is being exhibited by co-author Maria Andreoli and her helpers.

advanced level, the Utility, dogs compete for the title Utility Dog (UD). Classes are sub-divided into "A" (for beginners) and "B" (for more experienced handlers). A perfect score at any level is 200,

## A GENTLEMAN'S SPORT

Whether or not your dog wins top honors, showing is a pleasant social event. Sometimes, one may meet a troublemaker or nasty exhibitor, but these people should be ignored and forgotten. In the extremely rare case that someone threatens or harasses you or your dog, you can lodge a complaint with the hosting kennel club. This should be done with extreme prudence. Complaints are investigated seriously and should never be filed on a whim.

and a dog must score 170 or better to earn a "leg," of which three are needed to earn the title. To earn points, the dog must score more than 50% of the available points in each exercise; the possible points range from 20 to 40.

Each level consists of a different set of exercises. In the Novice level, the dog must heel on- and off-lead, come, long sit, long down and stand for examination. These skills are the basic ones required for a well-behaved "Companion Dog." The Open level requires that the dog perform the same exercises above but without a leash for extended lengths of time, as well as retrieve a dumbbell, broad jump and drop on recall. In the Utility level, dogs must perform ten difficult

Dog shows are enjoyable and educational experiences for young pups, like this Bergamasco youth who seems to be enjoying his day at the show.

points, which requires three first places in Open B and Utility under three different judges.

## AGILITY TRIALS

Having had its origins in the UK back in 1977, agility in the US traces to 1986, when the first organization to promote the sport in the US, the United States Dog Agility Association, Inc. (USDAA), was established. All dogs can compete, providing the dog is 18 months of age or older. Agility is designed so that the handler demonstrates how well the dog can work at his side. The handler directs his dog over an obstacle course that includes jumps (such as those used in the working trials), as well as tires, the dog walk, weave poles, pipe tunnels, collapsed tunnels, etc. While working his way through

exercises, including scent discrimination, hand signals for basic commands, directed jump and directed retrieve.

Once a dog has earned the UD title, he can compete with other proven obedience dogs for the coveted title of Utility Dog Excellent (UDX), which requires that the dog win "legs" in ten shows. Utility Dogs who earn "legs" in Open B and Utility B earn points toward their Obedience Trial Champion title. In 1977, the title Obedience Trial Champion (OTCh.) was established by the AKC. To become an OTCh., a dog needs to earn 100

### NO SHOW

Never show a dog that is sick or recovering from surgery or infection. Not only will this put your own dog under a tremendous amount of stress, but you will also put other dogs at risk of contracting any illness your dog has. Likewise, bitches who are in heat will distract and disrupt the performances of males who are competing, and bitches that are pregnant will likely be stressed and exhausted by a long day of showing.

the course, the dog must keep one eye and ear on the handler and the rest of his body on the course. The handler gives verbal and hand signals to guide the dog through the course.

Agility is great fun for dog and owner with many rewards for everyone involved. Interested owners should join a training club that has obstacles and experienced agility handlers who can introduce you and your dog to the "ropes" (and tires, tunnels, and so on).

## HERDING TESTS AND TRIALS

Breed clubs sponsor herding trials for Bergamascos that give the dogs an opportunity to test their natural herding skills. The handler works directly with his Bergamasco in an effort to herd livestock, including sheep, duck, cattle and goats. Owners interested in herding events should contact their breed club or the American Herding Breeds Association (AHBA), an organization founded in 1986 that assists owners of herding breeds. The main focus of AHBA is the working dog, though most dogs today are only "hobby herding dogs" (and do not do it to earn their daily biscuit).

The American Kennel Club (AKC) sanctions its own herding trials and tests and offers titles to dogs that succeed in these events. The titles include Herding

## SHOW-RING ETIQUETTE

Just as with anything else, there is a certain etiquette to the show ring that can only be learned through experience. Showing your dog can be quite intimidating to you as a novice when it seems as if everyone else knows what he is doing. You can familiarize yourself with ring procedure beforehand by taking showing classes to prepare you and your dog for conformation showing and by talking with experienced handlers. When you are in the ring, it is very important to pay attention and listen to the instructions you are given by the judge about where to move your dog. Remember, even the most skilled handlers had to start somewhere. Keep it up and you too will become a proficient handler as you gain practice and experience.

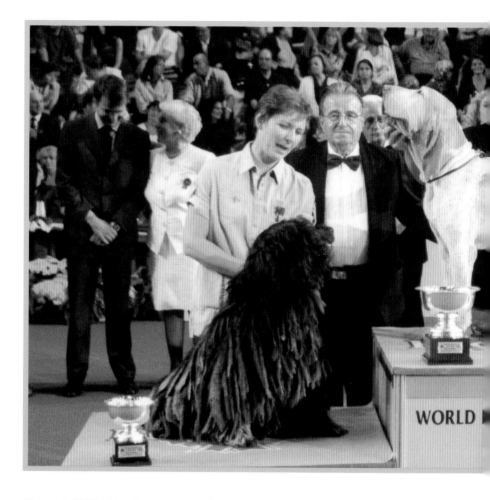

Started (HS), Herding Intermediate (HI) and Herding Excellent (HX), all of which are used as suffixes to the dog's name. The main title is a prefix and the most difficult to attain: Herding Champion (HC). The Bergamasco does not qualify to compete in these trials as the breed remains unrecognized by the American Kennel Club (AKC).

**WORKING TRIALS**

In England, working trials can be entered by any well-trained dog of any breed, not just Working dogs. Many dogs that earn The Kennel Club Good Citizen Dog award choose to participate in a working trial. There are five stakes at both Open and Championship levels: Companion Dog (CD), Utility Dog (UD), Working

An Italian sweep at the World Dog Show held in Milan, Italy, in 2000: the Bergamasco won third place, preceded by the Neapolitan Mastiff in second and the Bracco Italiano for Best in Show.

Dog (WD), Tracking Dog (TD) and Patrol Dog (PD). As in conformation shows, dogs compete against a standard and, if the dog reaches the qualifying mark, he obtains a certificate. The exercises are divided into groups, and the dog must achieve at least 70% of the allotted score for each exercise in order to qualify. If the dog achieves 80 percent in the Open level, he receives a Certificate of Merit (COM); in the Championship level, he receives a Qualifying Certificate.

Part of the qualifying exercises include Agility exercises, which consist of three jumps: a vertical scale up a wall of planks; a clear jump over a basic hurdle with a removable top bar; and a long jump across angled planks.

On the verge of world domination, the Bergamasco is growing in popularity around the world and can be seen at many international shows throughout Europe, America and beyond.

To earn the UD, WD and TD, dogs also must track approximately one-half mile for articles laid from one-half hour to three hours previously. Tracks consist of turns and legs, and fresh ground is used for each participant. The fifth stake, PD, involves teaching manwork, which is not recommended for every breed.

## FÉDÉRATION CYNOLOGIQUE INTERNATIONALE

Established in 1911, the Fédération Cynologique Internationale (FCI) represents the "world kennel club." This international body brings uniformity to the breeding, judging and showing of pure-bred dogs. Although the Fédération Cynologique Internationale originally included only five European nations: France, Germany, Austria, the Netherlands and Belgium (which remains its headquarters), the organization today embraces nations on six continents and recognizes well over 300 breeds of pure-bred dog.

The FCI sponsors both national and international shows. The hosting country determines the judging system and breed standards are always

### FCI FUNCTIONS
The FCI *does not* issue pedigrees. The FCI members and contract partners are responsible for issuing pedigrees and training judges in their own countries. The FCI does maintain a list of judges and makes sure that they are recognized throughout the FCI member countries.

The FCI also *does not* act as a breeder referral; breeder information is available from FCI-recognized national canine societies in each of the FCI's member countries.

based on the breed's country of origin. Dogs from every country can participate in these impressive canine spectacles, the largest of which is the World Dog Show, hosted in a different country each year.

There are three titles attainable through the FCI: the International Champion, which is the most prestigious; the International Beauty Champion, which is based on aptitude certificates in different countries; and the International Trial Champion, which is based on achievement in obedience trials in different countries.

In order for a dog to become an FCI Champion, the a dog must win three CACs (*Certificats d'Aptitude au Championnat*) at regional or club shows under three different judges who are breed specialists. The title of International Champion is gained by winning four CACIBs (*Certificats d'Aptitude au Championnat International de Beauté*), which are offered only at international shows, with at least a one-year lapse between the first and fourth award.

The FCI is divided into ten "Groups" in which the breeds are classified, with the Bergamasco competing in Group 1 for Sheepdogs and Cattledogs. At the World Dog Show, the following classes are offered for each breed: Puppy Class (6–9 months), Junior Class (9–18 months), Open Class (15 months or older) and Champion Class. A dog can be awarded a classification of Excellent, Very Good, Good, Sufficient and Not Sufficient. Puppies can be awarded classifications of Very Promising, Promising or Not Promising. Four placements are made in each class. After all sexes and classes are judged, a Best of Breed is selected. Other special groups and classes may also be shown. Each exhibitor showing a dog receives a written evaluation from the judge.

Besides the World Dog Show and other all-breed shows, you can exhibit your dog at specialty shows held by different breed clubs. Specialty shows may have their own regulations.

# INDEX

# My Bergamasco

PUT YOUR PUPPY'S FIRST PICTURE HERE

Dog's Name _____

Date _____ Photographer _____